The Rale Rasic Story

The Rale Rasic Story

as told to Ray Gatt

The Socceroos' First World Cup Coach

First published in Australia in 2006 by
New Holland Publishers (Australia) Pty Ltd
Sydney • Auckland • London • Cape Town

14 Aquatic Drive Frenchs Forest NSW 2086 Australia
218 Lake Road Northcote Auckland New Zealand
86 Edgware Road London W2 2EA United Kingdom
80 McKenzie Street Cape Town 8001 South Africa

10 9 8 7 6 5 4 3 2 1

National Library of Australia Cataloguing-in-Publication Data:

Rasic, Rale.
My world cup : the Rale Rasic story.
ISBN 1 74110 464 5.
1. Rasic, Rale. 2. Soccer coaches - Australia - Biography.
I. Gatt, Ray. II. Title.
796.334092

Publisher: Martin Ford
Editor: Jenny Hunter
Designer: Tania Gomes
Production Controller: Grace Gutwein
Printer: McPhersons's Printing Group

Cover photo: Rale Rasic at a promotion event at the 1974 World Cup in Germany

About the author

Ray Gatt was born in Balmain, Sydney in 1954. He grew up in Cabramatta and has lived all of his life in Sydney's south western suburbs. Ray went to Sacred Heart primary at Cabramatta before completing his senior education at Patrician Brothers College, Fairfield.

He became a cadet journalist with the *Daily Telegraph* in 1972.

His first assignment was covering an Ampol Cup match at Garside Park in Granville, but he specialised in horse racing before moving on to general sport in which he covered a host of sports including rugby league, cricket and soccer.

Ray joined the *Sydney Morning Herald* in 1980 as a racing writer but eventually found his way back into soccer as chief reporter in 1983. He joined the now defunct Sydney *Sun* in 1988 as chief soccer writer before it closed down four months later.

After a short stint at Australian Associated Press, Ray rejoined News Ltd and has now been chief soccer writer at the national daily, *The Australian* since 1989.

He is married to Karen and has a son, David. This is his first book.

Contents

Foreword by Kevin Sheedy

AS the 2006 soccer World Cup approaches it is usually around this time I reflect on what might have been in regards to my career as a coach. Strange as it may sound, I owe the round ball game and one man in particular, Rale Rasic, a debt of grattude, for had it not been for the 1974 Socceroos, I might well still be digging trenches and unblocking drains as a plumber.

It was the Socceroos who frightened the life out of Jack Hamilton and the late Alan Schwab, who were running Australian Football (the Victorian Football League at the time), when they qualified for the World Cup finals in Germany in a result many saw as the awakening of the Sleeping Giant of Australian sport. Until then Australian Football had been unchallenged as the number one winter sport in Melbourne.

Few fans, and certainly all forms of the media, had paid little attention to a code which struggled because of its strong ethnic ties and inability to connect with the mainstream Australian sporting community. But the winds of change were starting to blow, maybe not at hurricane proportions, but with enough of a breeze at its back to shake the complacency and lethargy out of the powers that be.

With the media showing interest in it and the number of kids taking up the game in school, soccer was now being viewed as some sort of threat. It was in this climate of apprehension that Australian Football officials asked my then club Richmond—where I was playing—to trial a new, ground-breaking position on its behalf: a development and promotions officer.

Armed with a 16mm projector, it was my job, with the help of a few others, to go around to various schools and clubs and spread the gospel of Australian Football. The rest is history.

For me Rale Rasic, who I class as a friend, stands as a great monument, not only to soccer in this country, but Australian sport in general. His achievements in the local game at both international and club level are almost iconic and there are few honours and rewards that have eluded him over a coaching career that has spanned 36 years. Rale's elevation to national coach at a young age represented the start of an amazing journey for him, a journey that had its origins in an orphanage in his homeland back in the early 1940s. His is an incredible story of determination, strength, vision and a will to succeed against the odds.

While Australian soccer is now basking in the glory of the Socceroos under Dutch coach Guus Hiddink, reaching the World Cup finals for the second time, Rale's role in the emergence of the sport here should never be forgotten. There is no doubting he was a great coach. He was tough and had the ability get the best out of his players. He was also clever enough to change the way the Socceroos played the game, combining the Australian way of physical attributes and strength with a touch of Europe thrown in.

Rale also had to deal with the heavy ethnic and British influence in the game at the time. Players were drawn from all parts of the world, yet he was able to mix a magnificent and special cocktail for success.

It should be remembered that Rale's feat of taking the Socceroos to the World Cup finals will never be bettered. I hear you ask 'what about Guus Hiddink's team?' Let's not forget that when the Socceroos qualified in 1974 they did so as one of the best 16 teams in the world, not one of the best 32 as it stands now.

It will always remain a mystery to me why the powerbrokers of the sport were so quick to dump him after the wonderful success of 1974. As a coach involved in a rival sport, I guess I should be thankful for the intervention of football politics, for that decision helped keep soccer way in the background.

As a lover of sport and a friend of Rale's, I say those responsible should look back on that decision with deep regret. Thankfully, Rale, as you would expect, has been strong enough to rise above it all—and the game is all the richer for that.

Introduction

You should write a book. How many times have I been told that over the years? While my family, friends, various Australian soccer players and work mates have continually been at me, I just didn't believe I had it in me.

Then, about six years ago, maybe longer, my good friend Rale Rasic, who I had first met in the early 1970s when I kicked off as a junior reporter with Sydney's *Daily Telegraph*, started pestering me. 'I am writing a book, can you provide me with a chapter?' he asked. He had also asked several other journalists, including the *Daily Telegraph's* John Taylor to do the same. To be honest, I thought it was a silly idea, not the book, but me and other journalists writing different chapters, but I didn't have the heart to tell Rale that it was not the way it should be done.

I kept putting him off and so did John, who also thought Rale was going about things the wrong way. Despite both of us getting regular telephone calls often starting with the words, 'You bastard, when are you going to write that chapter for me?' we managed to keep fobbing him off.

That is, until he finally broke me. After another of his calls, I told him it was silly the way he was approaching the book and that, even with my limited knowledge of the book business, no publisher would touch it. 'Look mate, I'll write it for you,' I said halfway through 2005. 'Would you? That would be marvelous,' he said. I suspect it was what he had been fishing for, for sometime, but Rale obviously wanted me to do it when I was good and ready. He was always big on psychology as you will discover when reading this book.

There was, however, one proviso if I was to write the book. Rale, whom I have known very closely since 1986, is a passionate man about anything he tackles. He can also talk under water and usually goes off on a hundred different tangents. One 'I'll only be two minutes' phone call or chat usually turns into an hour discussion in which he will circumnavigate the world and sort out the universe! 'Rale, when we sit down to do the book we will do it in an orderly fashion, chapter by chapter and there'll be no changing the subject or going in different tangents,' were my orders for him. 'Yes, my mate, yes, no worries.'

Stupid me! How long have I known him? Not only did he go off on different subjects, but it would take at least 40 minutes after arriving at his place to get started because I would get caught up looking at all the 1974 and other football memorabilia in his wonderful and comprehensive museum at the back of his house. Then again, I suppose that was my fault. I have seen it so many times, yet every time I went back I found something new and interesting.

I now wish I had been good and ready years ago to write the book for Rale's amazing story has gone untold for far too long. Having sat with him for countless hours there were many times when I was simply spellbound by his stories, though I had heard a few of them a myriad times before.

It is worth keeping in mind that this is not just a book about football, matches and the 1974 Socceroos. There were times when we both shed a tear, especially when he talked about his parents, the fact he cannot remember their faces as he has no mementos of his childhood because they were all destroyed during the war, the orphanage he grew up in and the effect his obsession with football and coaching had on his family life.

It is an inspirational story and I could not have written it without the help of a lot of people. My wonderful wife, Karen, and son, David, have been a huge support, putting up with me spending so much time with Rale and being on the computer until all hours of the morning. Karen's expertise with computers has been a godsend for this largely computer illiterate.

Then there is Ian Heads, a top class journalist, writer and a fine man, who I had the pleasure of working with at the *Daily Telegraph* during the 1970s. Ian eventually left newspaper reporting to launch a very successful career as an author. He was my first port of call when I decided to write Rale's book and his encouragement was greatly appreciated.

It was Ian who put me on to literary agent, Bruce Kennedy, who set the wheels in motion by finding a publisher and briefing me on the ins and outs of book publishing. He has been a wonderful help.

John Taylor, my best mate (along with Tony Labbozzetta, Les Scheinflug and the late Eddie Thomson) and a fine journalist in his own right, was left shaking his head when I told him I was writing Rale's book. 'You know what you are letting yourself in for, don't you?' he would say to me. Nonetheless John, who also gets on very well with Rale, gave me nothing but support and was a great help in reading the manuscript and providing information.

I'd like to acknowledge Fiona, Martin, Tania and all the people at New Holland for their support and superb expertise. They have made things so much easier for me.

I'd like to thank a good friend of Rale's, John Tscheppera, who did so much background work and provided substantial material for the book. John, who also did a great job in proofreading the manuscript, has a great love of the game and his efforts and his unselfishness are so typical of the man.

Finally, to Rale, who is a true mate and a legend, not only of Australian soccer, but sport in this country. Your young-at-heart philosophy, hunger for knowledge, passion for the game and everything else you do, dedication, encouragement and unrelenting worth ethic has been an inspiration for me.

Ray Gatt

Chapter 1

An Orphan's Life

Boom! Boom! Boom!

That awful, gut-wrenching, horrific sound of bombs exploding. They may have been emanating from a distance but, for a five-year-old, they may as well have been going off in our backyard. So close, so frightening. Some things never leave you.

This is one of my earliest recollections of my youth in Mostar, where I was brought into a world of hate and conflict in 1935 and, crazy as it may seem, these days I can still remember the explosions, the fireballs and the brutality but not the faces of my parents.

The good times, the joys of youth, the love and the warmth every child deserves to experience were viciously and cruelly ripped from me, stolen by a monster I could hear and feel almost every day but could not see.

Yes, times were tough in Mostar and the drama and fighting brought about by both the ethnic tensions and world situation of the time were just part of the every day life for the people of the town.

Mostar was, and still is, an extraordinary town in every sense of the word. It was said that Mostar was not only a mosaic of cultures and traditions, but a real melting pot of them. It consisted of

Bosniaks (the replacement name for the Muslim population so as to avoid religious confusion), Serbs and Croats with predominantly Muslim, Orthodox and Roman Catholic religions and a population that spoke Bosnian, Croatian or Serbian.

Mostar has a wonderful Mediterranean-style climate, which makes it one of the warmest cities in Bosnia-Herzegovina. The fertile grounds bordering the Neretva River, which is regarded as one of the coldest rivers in the world, produces a rich harvest of cherries, grapes, figs, mandarins and lemons, as well as some of the finest red and white wines in the country. There you can fish for some of the most delicious and intelligent trout in the world.

I know this through reading books and the internet because, apart from my vague recollections of the bombs and fighting, I know little about my very early days.

I was the second of four children (two girls, Ivanka and Katarina and two boys, myself and Dragoslav) born to Ivan and Stanislava. I can't even remember the faces of my parents. I don't have photographs or mementos because most of our possessions were destroyed; my parent's lives are somewhat of a mystery to me.

I know dad was born around Mostar. He was a book-keeper and was forced to travel around the country to earn a meagre living. It was on one of his trips that he met my mother, who was born to a Montenegrin family.

Not surprisingly, it was left to mum, the dedicated housewife, to maintain some sort of family order and I shudder to think how difficult it must have been for her with four kids to look after.

That, unfortunately, is the sum total of my knowledge of my parents. I don't remember at what point they disappeared from my life.

According to my late sister Ivanka, who passed away in 1973, my father was an organiser with the partisan movement in our area. He was killed in the last days of the Second World War—none of us knew how he died. Sometimes it is best that some things are left alone.

For some reason, I have recollections of my uncle Milan, who was a very tall man at over six foot, three inches. With my father away most of the time, I seemed to spend more time at his place, which was on the outskirts of Mostar and about 15 kilometres from home.

Uncle Milan, who was a loving and easy-going person, was married but had no kids and I think I was just about his adopted son. I formed a wonderful bond with him and the fact that there were wide, open fields near his house which allowed me to have great fun playing with the neighbourhood kids made for many special moments.

But tragedy soon struck and my life was turned upside down.

I was devastated when I discovered that uncle Milan had been killed. It was in the early 1940s when the ethnic conflict, which had been gathering strength, was compounded by World War 2.

To this day I don't know what happened to my uncle, except that his was a brutal killing. This kind, wonderful man did not deserve such a fate. There was now more upheaval in my life as the world started to tear itself apart through war. As a result of his death, and at the age of about four and a half, I was whisked off to a local orphanage, which was home to about 30 children, while my father went off to be involved as an organizer of the partisan movement. Initally, my mother looked after my sisters before it became too much for her and they were placed in orphanages as well.

I was separated from my brother and sisters. Katarina, who was one, and Ivanka, who was seven, went to different orphanages round different parts of the country. Dragoslav was the lucky one. He was born in 1944—some four years after Katarina, Ivanka and myself were sent to the orphanges. I did not even know he existed. He was adopted by a family from Dardar, near Osijek, which is now part of Croatia. It was wonderful that he was given a great upbringing in a family atmosphere.

My parents seemed to disappear from the face of the earth and I learned later that my mother had been brutally beaten and died in 1945, shortly after the birth of Dragoslav.

The ethnic war had started in 1939 and war came to the Kingdom of Yugoslavia on April 6 1941 as German forces swept south to support Mussolini's dreams of conquest. The Axis target was Greece, but they could only get there through Yugoslavia.

Barely two weeks after the Germans crossed the border, the Yugoslavian army capitulated. The ethnic tension that was simmering prior to the invasion accelerated and this, plus the impending arrival of the Germans, made life untenable for the people of Mostar, especially the younger ones.

A decision was made to evacuate the 30 children in the orphanage further away from the conflict.

You can only imagine how we felt as we were uprooted from the place of our birth, away from family and friends. Scared, distraught and fearful. Not knowing what lay ahead for us.

We boarded a train for Belgrade, 30 kids and one adult supervisor, and shuttled across the country for three or four days. At the end of the first day we ended up in a small orphanage in Sarajevo, the capital of Bosnia. The first thing that hit me was the cold. It was freezing. My teeth were chattering.

We stayed a few days before leaving for what was to be our final destination, Belgrade, the capital of Yugoslavia, where we were placed in an orphanage called Centralni Lazaret.

Centralni Lazaret was where orphans were evaluated, processed and directed to other more permanent orphanages throughout Belgrade and the neighbouring countryside.

Now, some people have different ideas based on what they have seen in the movies about orphanages. They are supposed to be grim, desperate, hellholes for the unwanted, misfits and the like.

But let me tell you, this was almost paradise on earth for me.

My favourite recollection of this place was that I was given new clothes, sit-down meals and was able to take showers with soap. What a luxury!

Centralni Lazaret was located opposite the home stadium of OFK Belgrade, the famous football club. We spent days playing various sports, but football was always top of the list.

Eventually, it was time to move on again after being processed. Again, I was struck with fear not knowing where I would end up. Would the next place be as good as this one?

As it turned out, I didn't have to worry. I ended up in a place I will always remember as my dream house. The orphanage was based on the banks of the Begej River in the town of Zrenjanin, some 50 kilometres from Belgrade and I would spend the best part of 10 or so wonderful years there, growing from a child until I eventually went off into the brave new world at the age of 17.

You could not have asked for a better environment. The Begej was always a hive of activity. It had a beautiful bathing beach—it was no Bondi, but served its purpose—provided for many water sports and had fantastic fish markets and a colourful and busy promenade.

Of course, the thing that caught my eye was the wide, open spaces surrounding the orphanage and, in particular, the football fields. While the grounds did not have grass covering, it did not stop us from pretending to be our football idols during countless hours of games.

And, as you would expect, ball games led to accidents. I recall that most of the windows on the first three floors of the orphanage were smashed by the over-zealous kicking of different sized balls. Once the culprits were discovered, the punishment was usually hard, but fair.

Despite the almost idyllic life, my thoughts continually drifted to my family. Barely a day went by when I did not think of them or long for them. I was not to know that I would never see my mother and father again. My brother and sisters were separated towards the end of the war. Dragoslav was adopted by a family in Osijek, and Ivanka and Katarina were sent to an orphanage in Vojvodina.

The orphanage, however, helped me immensely to get over my pain. There was no substitute for home and family, but this was the next best thing. It was run by the government and everything was done to give us the care we needed and the best opportunity to succeed in life.

The orphanage ended up producing many remarkable and successful people, including scientists, engineers and, of course, footballers.

I shared a room with a guy called Milan Galic who, at 16, became one of the youngest players to play in the second division with Proleter. He captained the Yugoslav team that won the gold medal at the 1960 Rome Olympics and eventually captained the full senior side.

There is absolutely no doubt that the orphanage shaped my life, on and off the football field, forever. I learned discipline. I learned that in life you do everything for yourself. I learned independence. I learned humility. I learned about having respect for yourself. I learned there is no substitute for education and, above all, I learned you had to be street-wise or you could not exist.

I also learned how to play chess, something that would hold me in good stead in my later years as a coach. Patience and discipline were things that were instilled in to me by my chess teacher. I had to think and plan four and five moves ahead, a good trait for a coach.

While life at the orphanage was spartan and disciplined and everything regimented it was nonetheless enjoyable. I have vivid memories of the daily regimen we, as kids, undertook.

We began our day very early. We'd make our beds, checked our wardrobes, which were numbered, mine was 101, to make sure our meagre possessions were in place. That's why the number 101 has a special place in my life, even today. Whenever I see that number, I flash back and the memories of the orphanage start to flow.

Eventually we would head off for our daily exercise—rain, hail or shine. We'd then go down to the river to splash our faces before going back to shower and breakfast and take part in the worst moment of the day. It was compulsory for every kid to have a spoonful of cod liver oil before breakfast. We were told it was for medicinal purposes. To be honest, I have not had any serious health problems over the years, so maybe it did do me some good!

School was compulsory, of course. The schoolhouse was just a brief walk down the road. The school day was divided into a morning and afternoon session. After breakfast we would line up in true military fashion and be led to school by an older child. Homework was done after a huge and impressive lunch at the orphanage.

While it was usually a long day, I remember we always kept going because of what we had to look forward to—dinner. Dinner was the best time and it usually made me feel like a king. This was heaven on earth for me and the rest of the kids. As weird as it may sound, we were, in fact, far better off than the kids in town.

Soup—vegetable, chicken or other—was compulsory followed by respectable helpings of veal, pork, potatoes, beans, cabbage, salads, powdered eggs and lots of home-cooked bread. There was also plenty of fruit on offer—apples, cherries, pears and watermelon.

By the end of a tough day we were always ready for bed. We'd wash up, clean our teeth, have a little chat amongst ourselves and then sleep like babies.

Playtime for us was also an exciting and joyous time. Sport and exercise were widely encouraged by the teachers. We played at every opportunity—volleyball, basketball, anything to do with balls. But one sport was a religion—football, the world game.

Whenever it was playtime, there would be a mad scramble for a piece of space to organise a game. It became common practice to nominate someone to stand near the door so that when the bell went, he would charge off and claim a piece of space for his group.

It didn't always work, however. Older boys would come along and kick us off. It was then we learned that discretion was the better part of valour. Losing a patch of dirt was not worth a bloodied nose or losing a few teeth!

The most important rule you learned, however, was that the kid who owned the ball was your friend. He often handpicked his team, so it was best to stay on his good side. You usually ended up on the best side as well and would rarely lose.

While the orphanage could never afford proper balls, it was usually a simple matter, and an art form, to make one. This involved negotiating with the local kids to get bladders, which were not available all year round.

They were more readily available before the New Year celebrations when the families slaughtered the home-grown pigs for their feast. New Year, and not Christmas, was always the main celebration. You have to remember that religion was not encouraged at the time.

Once we got the bladders, we would then get the thread from our woollen socks and wind it around it before cutting strips from sheets, wrapping them around the bladder and tying them up. We'd then rub dirt into it to give it a more authentic look.

We made footballs, volleyballs and tennis balls this way and they were the source of many memorable and life-shaping moments.

Chapter 2
Football

THE orphanage was a blessing for me, though I probably did not realise it at the time. It was my chance at a new life, a hideaway, a haven from the harsh reality of war and a pathway to success few of us would have dared dream about. It was like living in another world.

What more could I ask? What more could I hope for? The answer, before too long, became fairly obvious for me. Soccer. Football. Call it what you like, the language of the sport is the same all around the world.

The 'beautiful game' was always going to be a lure for me. It drove me and it consumed me, but I don't know that I saw it as my path to success. It wasn't like it is today, where kids seem to make up their minds that they will follow a particular path and it is going to lead them to something great, to fame and fortune.

As good as the orphanage was, and as good as the people who ran it were, the reality was that we were the forgotten ones, the disadvantaged. The real world was outside our boundaries where children grew up in mostly loving family environments, where kids got that extra bit of special attention and where they were given the best chance of succeeding.

As I said, the orphanage was a wonderful and unforgettable part of my life. It was a saviour. But it was no substitute for your real family. There was no father or mother to tuck you into bed and kiss you goodnight. No holding your hand or wiping your brow or face when you were sick. No long, loving hugs.

The orphanage, however, made up for it in other areas such as discipline, self-reliance, health, fitness and education. Not surprisingly, part of the culture of the orphanage was competition. It didn't matter in what form it came. General knowledge quizzes, mathematic contests, chess, swimming, running, football…it was always there.

It was a healthy part of our upbringing. It instilled spirit, teamwork, achievement and an overwhelming sense of beating the odds. Competition was greatly encouraged and usually involved different classes of the same age group.

If it wasn't enough that you were motivated by pride to do well in these competitions, the offer of various rewards such as theatre tickets, trips in to the city and special food treats added even more spice.

While the quizzes were terrific and added to your knowledge, the fiercest competitions were, of course, reserved almost totally for the football field. It didn't matter what type of football—the street variety, three-on-three or four-on-four—all games were treated like life and death.

The orphanage also had organised competitions where the boys were divided into teams and a league was established. The same happened at school. There were various leagues being played among the boys.

We were fortunate at the orphanage because games were also organised against local junior club sides such as Banat, Ecka, Zeljeznicar and Proleter, a club that was to eventually play a huge role in my career as a player.

The orphanage side eventually started to gain a reputation as a very good team, especially after beating Banat 14-0 and Proleter 6-0. We did not concede a goal in six straight matches and even the people of the town started to talk about us.

Of course, the news spread quickly and it wasn't long before the talent scouts started popping up, especially those involved with Proleter, a second division club in the area.

I excelled as a midfielder and I attracted the attention of the Proleter scouts. In 1949, at the age of 13, I joined my first professional club as a fullback and it changed my life. But I wasn't the only one for the orphanage produced many fine players.

They included Mihajlo Djuricin, who played for Proleter then graduated to the Yugoslavian national under 18s team in 1953, and Milan Galic, who went on to become one of the greatest strikers Yugoslavia produced. Galic was a superstar. He played for Proleter, Partizan Belgrade and Standard Liege (Belgium). He only recently retired as the lawyer of the Yugoslav Football Federation.

I'll never forget my first training session for Proleter. The club employed its own bootmaker—no commercially made boots were available at the time—and it was his responsibility to ensure every player had a pair of well-made and well-fitted boots. His was a precise job right down to the length of the studs – long for wet grounds and short for dry.

Newly arrived younger players were given hand-me-down boots and I was over the moon when I was given mine. However, while the boots fitted snugly, I soon discovered a nail was sticking through the sole of the right boot. But I wasn't game to complain.

I trained through my entire first session on my toes and in terrible pain, but my intuition told me not to say a word. Eventually I was given a brand new pair of boots just before I played my first game for the club.

These were more great times for me. Football was now my passion and not only was I playing for Proleter, but also for the orphanage and the school. I loved the regimen involved with my football.

I would walk to school in the morning, return to the orphanage for lunch, do some study then go off to training with Proleter. This was a real eye-opener for me. We trained five times a week and it was usually done in daylight because there were no such things as floodlights. We would train for two hours or until the sun went down.

Summer was the easiest time to train. During winter the weather was freezing and we would have to contend with snow. The sun usually went down at 3.30pm so we would then go to the gymnasium. I dare say the sort of training we did in the gym would have been ground-breaking stuff.

I revelled in it all. I was becoming somewhat of a star with the orphanage and the school, and the club encouraged me. The club was very good to the orphanage and school, a fantastic benefactor. Of course, the club always came first so once I made first grade, I could not play for the orphanage or the school any more.

It wasn't until 1952, when I was 16, that I really caught the eye of the Proleter coaches and started to make limited appearances in the first team during friendlies and Cup games. That only came about after going through the usual initiation process which involved playing in an inter-club, Possibles v Probables game.

The senior players were always told to go in hard against the youngsters and newly arrived players. My goodness, they were very tough games and only the strongest and mentally prepared survived. I saw many good, talented players fall by the wayside because they simply could not cope. It was a harsh way of doing things, but it sorted the men from the boys.

I played one of my first games for the club in a friendly against Vojvodina in Zrenjanin in November 1952 and we lost 3–1. I played as a right fullback, a position I was to play in for most of my career.

The year 1952 will also stay close to my heart for other reasons. Having been separated from my brother and sisters, I just did not know where they were or even if they were still alive.

With the help of the Red Cross, Ivanka, who was in an orphanage house in Vojvodina, started to look for her family. One day she noticed in the local newspaper that a player called Rale Rasic was making a name playing for Proleter.

The media had inadvertently done its job. Ivanka finally made contact with the club. After 12 years apart, we finally met up in Subotica where Proleter was playing in a youth tournament. Just waiting to see her again left me a total emotional wreck. I could hardly think of anything else. So you can imagine the outpouring of emotion when we got to hug and hold each other again. A tiny part of my life had been returned.

The job was not finished, however. Ivanka and I made a concerted effort to find the rest of the family. My selection in the Yugoslav under 18s side helped speed up the search and, in 1953, we found Katarina and two years later we finally tracked down Dragoslav.

Piece by piece the family had been reunited and we finally all got together in 1955 in Zrenjanin for the first time since 1940. What a joyous and wonderful moment it was. I could not believe it was happening because I truly never thought I would see my family again.

Tears flowed and we hugged and hugged like never before. We just held on to each other for hours and hours, afraid to let go for fear someone or something would tear us apart again.

Now I was on top of the world. With my family back from the dead and my football going great guns, things could not have been better for me.

In 1953 Proleter played against the mighty Red Star, a club known throughout the world, in a friendly, and while we lost 4–

2, the match will remain as one of my most memorable.

Cracking first grade was still tough but I was enjoying playing in the youth side anyway because we had a superb team, coached by a guy called Koca Kolarov, who was in charge of what was regarded as one of the greatest youth programs in Yugoslavia.

Kolarov was a fantastic coach who knew the game inside out. He was revered by everyone at Proleter, especially the younger players who absolutely idolised him. Apart from his skills as a coach, he was simply one of the nicest men you would ever wish to meet.

Under his guidance, the club produced seven Yugoslav under 18s and senior international players—not bad for a second division club.

Playing for the youth side and under Kolarov was an experience and a half. In the 1952–53 season we participated in a series of tournaments to find the best youth team in Yugoslavia. It was a long and tough road.

We started by winning our provincial play-offs before qualifying for the state finals, where we eventually beat Vojvodina 9–0 in Novisad. That took us to the national championship play-offs, where we played against the big guns like Red Star and OFK Belgrade. We were eventually crowned the best youth side in the country.

Of course, our performances really caught the eye of our club and, eventually, seven players from that squad went on to play first grade that season.

My first full senior debut came against Smederevo in a league home game in a match we won 1–0. I'll never forget it because I was told I had to mark a player I had always admired—Tom Stankovic.

He was five foot nothing and was bow-legged but boy, could he play. All week at training our coach was at me about him. What to look for and what to do and not to do. 'He has more tricks in his feet than you've ever seen before,' the coach warned me.

You can imagine I was a nervous wreck by the time the game started and I was all at sea for the first 10 minutes. It was a real battle but I am proud to say I recovered well and marked Stankovic to perfection.

Having survived that experience, it wasn't long before I became a regular member of the senior team and, with that, I was no longer allowed to play for the orphanage or the school team. Life was starting to move quickly for me.

My next big step in 1953 was selection, along with fellow orphan, Mihajlo Djuricin, who was also in the Proleter first team, in the Yugoslav national under 18s squad for a tournament in Belgium in 1953. As you can imagine, that news was greeted with amazing celebrations by the orphanage and the general community. We were big time now!

I came on as a substitute in three games and we finished runners-up, losing the final to a very good Hungarian side.

In 1954, I was again selected for the national under 18s to play in the UEFA national championships in Bonn, Germany. This was a huge thrill for me because our team was coached by a legend of Yugoslav football, Djokica Vujadinovic, who played in the first FIFA World Cup finals in 1930 when Yugoslavia lost 6–1 in the semi-final to hosts and eventual champions, Uruguay.

We comprehensively beat Ireland 4–1 in our first match before beating East Germany 4–1 then losing 2–1 to Spain. Despite losing to Spain we still progressed to the semi-finals where we lost to a great Hungarian side 2–0 on April 6. While it was disappointing to lose, it was a superb effort by us to get so far.

After the tournament we travelled back home by train and while I was still over the moon with having been involved in the tournament, things were going to get a lot better for me.

At the time there were no such things as player agents and written contracts were few and far between. But no sooner had the train pulled into the station in Belgrade – the squad was having a one-day layover—than I was approached by representatives from first division club Vojvodina.

It was an offer too good to refuse. The club wanted me to go with them immediately to their headquarters in Novisad, but I refused. I just wanted to get home to the orphanage and share my wonderful experiences with everyone there.

I am glad I did. When we got back there were amazing scenes. The orphanage, the school and the town were all basking in the glory of what their orphans had achieved in the tournament in Germany. The local newspapers were full of stories about Kolarov's Babes. Everyone was just so proud.

Going back also gave me a chance to say goodbye to the only home I had ever really known. I spent the best part of 14 years at the orphanage, about a fifth of my life. It was extremely difficult to say goodbye, to leave behind the many friends I had made, to leave behind the security and love of a truly amazing little world of its own.

To this day, the orphanage is still deeply and affectionately embedded in me. I have carried a large slice of it in my heart throughout my fortunate life. It will remain with me until my last breath.

As hard as it was to walk out the gate of the orphanage for the last time, I knew I could not look back. There was no turning back for me. A new and exciting chapter in my life was opening for this orphan.

Chapter 3

I'm No Superstar

As I headed to Vojvodina, myriad thoughts went through my mind. What lay ahead for me? How would I cope without the security of orphanage life? Could I make it in the big time? So many questions, so few answers.

When I finally arrived in Vojvodina in the middle of 1954, I was met by the club's officials and taken by car to the Hotel Vojvodina in Novisad, where I was to spend the next week getting acclimatised to my new surrounds and the different way of life.

Understandably, this was a whole, new, crazy world for me. The hotel used to be known as the Queen Jeliseveta, then the Queen Maria and then the Hotel Vojvodina but the name did not matter for it was absolute luxury for me. It was where a lot of footballers, movie people, writers and academics stayed and here I was mixing with some of them. I felt like I was in the movies!

This place was as far removed from the orphanage as you could imagine, but still, some habits die hard. Every morning I made sure the bed was made and the room was neat and tidy. I remember one day the maid came in to the room to go about her business and she started shaking her head.

'This room is always neat and tidy. You know you don't have to do anything, it is my job to clean up. Why do you do it?" she said somewhat incredulously.

While some people would probably think twice about giving away their background, especially if they were brought up in an orphanage or led a tough, underprivileged life, I had no such qualms.

'I was brought up in an orphanage and this is the way we did things," I said proudly.

Another new experience for me was the fact that everything from meals to drinks was provided free of charge. I simply had to sign for it and the bill was picked up by the club. But to be honest, I never took too much advantage of it. If only those at the orphanage could see me now!

The hotel was in the centre of Novisad and only a 15-minute walk to the stadium for training and games. Novisad was the capital and cultural hub of Vojvodina, which is one of the most developed provinces of Serbia.

Vojvodina lies on the Pannonian Plain at the convergence of the Danube, Tisa and Sava rivers. The region has a magnificent cultural background with numerous theatres and cultural societies that foster folk dancing and music from all ethnic groups. There are galleries and showrooms sprawled throughout the province.

Vojvodina is also steeped in a sporting tradition that can be traced back to the middle of the 19th century. For such a small region, it achieved remarkable results internationally and nationally in football, basketball and volleyball.

For me, being a part of that tradition was awe inspiring. I could hardly believe this was happening to me.

Football-wise, I was like a kid in a lolly shop. Vojvodina had nine full internationals in its squad, including Todor Veselinovic, Vujadin Boskov and Aleksandar Ivos and to be within touching distance of them would have been a privilege and eye-opener let alone mixing with them as a team-mate!

Veselinovic was a striker who also played for Partizan and the national team as well as coaching Olympiakos in Greece and later the Yugoslavian national team. Boskov was one of Yugoslavia's greatest players and also represented the World XI as a midfielder. He coached Vojvodina, Italy's Sampdoria and Roma, Spain's Real Madrid and the national team. Ivos was a midfielder who eventually became Vojvodina's technical director and was sought after by many other clubs as the head of football.

I became great friends with Todor and our paths crossed again many decades later when he brought Olympiakos to Australia in 1978. I was coaching the NSW side at the time and the Greeks taught us a lesson and beat us 4–1.

Of course, being a new player at such a big club, things were never going to be easy for me at Vojvodina. Matters were not helped by the fact that, under the rules of the day, I had to serve a sort of apprenticeship before I was allowed to play in a league or cup game for the club.

The rules, which were the same for all players around the country, stated a player transferring to a new club had to wait three months before he could play in a friendly and six months before he could play in a League or Cup match.

Much of my early days there were made up of training and playing in pick-up matches organised for the senior players to test the mettle of the newcomers.

At one end of the club's stadium was a *kuca* (house) which was used by the players to get changed before and after training. Directly in front of the building was a red gravel area, approximately 30 metres square where the likes of Veselinovic, Boskov and Ivos organised small-sided contests as well as one touch and piggy-in-the-middle games, usually before training and sometimes on our day off.

It was a tremendous grounding for me and the other younger players. We learned so much from that tough initiation. I called it street football and I believe it helped define much of my character in later life.

One of the best moments in the early stages was the time the national under 18s came into camp in Novisad. It was the same team I had played for two years before. The latest lot included my friend Milan Galic and the legendary Dragoslav Sekularac.

At the age of 12, Sekularac was already involved in playing in curtain raisers for Red Star Belgrade. He was such a super talent that the fans would often give him a standing ovation. By the time he was 16 he had become a regular first team player with Red Star and regarded as one of the greatest young prospects in world football.

He, of course, went on to play for Yugoslavia, earning one of the greatest compliments by being dubbed Europe's White Pele. Sekularac became an accomplished coach, who won the league-cup double with Red Star before coaching in South America.

Dragoslav came out to Australia in the 1980s and coached Footscray, becoming NSL coach of the year. He returned overseas before coming back to Melbourne to coach Heidelberg to the NSL Cup final in which the Victorians beat my side, Parramatta Eagles, with the last kick of the match. I hated losing, but losing to him made it just a little bit easier to take.

We have been firm friends since 1952.

My first 'game' for Vojvodina was against the Yugoslav national under 18s. But little was I to know that my time at the club would be relatively brief, a mere eight memorable months.

I believe I would have walked into the first grade side had that silly 'apprenticeship' rule not been around. Unfortunately, I found things difficult. Without the real competitive edge of first team football, those outside the first team lost so much touch and physical and mental sharpness. We also missed the excitement and pressure of playing in front of big crowds.

As fate would have it, I never got to play first grade, though I played in six friendlies, and a continuing turn of events eventually ended my association with the club.

One of the friendlies will stay in my memory. Three months after the transfer to Vojvodina I was supposed to play in a match against Proleter Osijek (not my old club) in Osijek. Unbeknown to me, my brother Dragoslav, who was 10 at the time, was taken to the match by the man who had adopted him when he was just a baby. The father, who was named Lazar, read about me in the newspaper and took Dragoslav along in the hope of meeting me. What a wonderful gesture by the man.

We were warming up behind the goal during the curtain raiser to our match and Lazar attracted my attention and introduced me to this kid. 'This is your brother,' he said. I was speechless at first, then overtaken by tremendous emotion. It was the first time I had seen him since we had been separated. I gave Dragoslav a huge hug and the coach saw what was going on. He came over and asked what was going on and I explained the situation.

He simply told me to go back to the dressing room, get showered and changed and told me to go and spend time with my brother. I was overwhelmed. That was a remarkable piece of humanity from the coach. Of course, at that stage, I was desperate to get into the first team, but that did not matter at that stage. I had got my brother back.

These days we are close, not as close as we could have been, but close enough. I brought him to Australia around 1969 when he was about 25. He has done very well for himself. He is an industrial chemist, travels and lectures all over the world and is vice president for UBIS Asia, a technical company for industrial chemistry. Dragoslav and his wife Teresa have lived in Bangkok for the past 20 years.

Sadly, Ivanka, who had done so much to get the family together again, died at the young age of 39. She had a young family and left two very young kids (Dragoslav and Svetlana). I won't go into the details except to say her death was the culmination of the suffering she endured for most of her life.

Katarina now lives in Sydney with her husband Matias after arriving here in 1969.

The straw that broke the camel's back regarding me leaving Vojvodina, which was experiencing an injury crisis at the time, came when a guy called Novak Roganovic was promoted to the side at right back—my position—for a match. At that stage he was being tipped to be transferred to another club. Sadly, I was still stymied by the six-month rule so I had to sit in the stands.

As fate would have it, Roganovic played the game of his life. He starred in the 4–1 win over Spartak and his life changed forever after that. He eventually became a member of the Yugoslav gold medal team at the 1960 Olympics and represented the national team many times.

With other players coming back from injury and Roganovic secure in his position, there was no more room for me at Vojvodina and I was transferred to FK Spartak in Subotica.

They were the breaks, but I held no grudges and certainly none towards Roganovic, who was to become a good friend. Football and sport is about being in the right place at the right time and taking your chances. I was sure my turn would come.

I transferred to Spartak in the summer of 1955 and I was to enjoy my best times as a footballer at this club.

Spartak is situated in Subotica, which lies in the very northern part of Yugoslavia, about 60 kilometres from the border with Hungary in the heart of the Pannonian Plain. Subotica is situated on an ancient watershed system between vast sandy areas in the north and the diluvial Aeolian plateau in the south.

Subotica was first mentioned in a 14th century document as Zobodka and, since then, has been called by over 200 different names. The name Subotica first appeared in 1653.

It was in Subotica, which I would call my second dream home, where my football career blossomed. Make no mistake, Spartak was a very successful club with huge influence not only on the national scene, but internationally as well. It was heavily influenced by Hungarian football.

I loved the fact that Spartak had a comprehensive international program that included trips to Hungary, Czechoslovakia, Austria, Bulgaria and East Germany.

Being at such a big club meant a huge change in attitude and in the way things were done. I remember my first pre-season was hellish and brutal. I had never been through anything like it before or since.

For three weeks we trained in the mountains, taking advantage of the high altitude, fresh air, steep mountains and few distractions. We also played some friendlies against much weaker opposition before happily returning to town and a more normal lifestyle.

There was never any rest, even during the mid-season break when we were required to go in to the mountains again for another three weeks of torture. This time we had to contend with snow that was knee deep at times.

Despite the wet and cold we had to stick to the daily routine which was an early morning endurance run in the snow, gymnastics, acrobatics and ball work at about 11.30 then another fitness session in the afternoon.

Spartak was a very successful club and was always perched in the first division. It produced many famous players, none more so than Bata Ognjanov, who also went on to play for Red Star before returning to Spartak. He was a national team player and idol of Yugoslavian football. Short and stocky, he was a remarkable header of the ball and it was often said that when Bata played, Spartak played.

I had many memorable moments during my five-year stay at the club, including our 3–1 win over Hajduk in Split, a 4–4 draw with Hungary's Honved in Subotica, a 4–4 league draw against Dinamo Zagreb, a Yugoslavian Cup quarter-final loss against Partizan Belgrade and a friendly against the Hungarian national team.

It was heart-breaking drawing with Dinamo who went through unbeaten in that season of 1958–59. We led 4–3 with just seconds to go and the radio and television stations were already proudly pronouncing a famous home victory for us until Dinamo equalised in stoppage time.

The Cup quarter-final against Partizan was remarkable. We led 2–1 before the scores finished locked at 3–3, forcing extra time. Sadly, Partizan grabbed the winner in the 119th minute—and the scorer? None other than my great mate from the orphanage, Milan Galic!

In 1958, Spartak got to play the Hungarian national team in a warm up match in the world famous Nep Stadium in Budapest just before the World Cup finals in Sweden. Well, you wouldn't believe it, but we led 2–1 with only 18 minutes to go and we were on a high.

Then reality struck. The Hungarians clicked into another gear and away they went. They put five past us before we knew what was happening. It was mesmerising stuff. I remember our goalkeeper, Gloncak, was so distraught after the match that he announced he was retiring.

While the 1959–60 season started with much promise and hope, it would end up being a disaster and was to be my last at Spartak. Just before Christmas 1959, we travelled to Dresden in

East Germany for an annual tournament which we had won the previous year. Four teams took part, Spartak, Dinamo Dresden, Lodz (Poland) and Dinamo Berlin.

It was a nightmare tournament. The conditions were atrocious with the temperature more than 10 degrees below freezing, the playing surface was like concrete and there was ice everywhere. It didn't help that the players wore aluminium studs!

My career took a turn for the worse five minutes before half-time in our opening game against Dresden when some bastard slid in and collected me on the right knee. Blood poured from the wound and I was in agony. I knew some serious damage had been done but, because it was so cold, the wound started to close up and I made it to halftime.

The coach checked the wound and said there was nothing wrong with me and told me to go out for the second half. There were no substitutes allowed at the time so I did as I was told. I finished the game but was in awful pain in the dressing room. Eventually it was discovered I had suffered ligament damage. That was the end for me for much of the season.

After three months in plaster, I recovered in time to play in the final stages of the season, but while I was never the same player again I did play an important representative match for Eastern Division against Western Division 1 and was lucky enough to be voted man-of-the-match. And that opened up another football opportunity for me.

I used my time out of football well, spending it on studying. Thankfully, the education mantra that was pumped in to me in my orphanage days kicked in and I was smart enough to realise that playing football was never going to be a lucrative profession for me. I needed something else to back me up later in life.

I made a conscious effort to broaden my education while I played football, so I undertook studies at various universities in whatever spare time I had. I have to admit, there was another ulterior motive as it also helped to stop me from being drafted into the army for my compulsory national service!

While I passed about 10 exams before leaving Yugoslavia, I had not yet attained a degree. It was something that played on my mind and I was to eventually rectify the situation.

As for my football, that representative game had attracted scouts from all over the place and, as a result of my performance, the technical director of FK Borac Banja Luka offered me a very good contract. I joined them for the 1960–61 season.

I had never seen so much money, but I was to discover that money wasn't everything. When I arrived at Borac, I was shocked by the facilities. The dressing room floors were wooden and oiled. They smelled and there were no spas and getting clean towels was always a challenge.

Needless to say, I did not enjoy my time at the club though there was one memorable match when we beat Velez Mostar 6–2 in the Bosnia-Herzegovina Cup. I did not know it at the time, but it was to be my last visit to my birthplace.

Chapter 4

Australia and a New Challenge

IT wasn't long before I became disillusioned with Borac. It wasn't what I wanted. The culture, the football, nothing appealed to me. I wanted a better challenge.

To be honest, I still thought I could play at a reasonable level. I was only 26 and figured I had a few good years ahead of me. I did not want to waste these important years, so I turned to a player-agent for some help at the end of the 1960–61 season while visiting Belgrade to continue with my university studies.

I loved being in Belgrade. I enjoyed the culture, the café scene, being with friends, chatting, eating and generally having fun. It was good to watch the various celebrities, movie stars, singers and footballers move around the place. Yes, I was in my element!

It was during a gathering at a local café that I met this player-agent, though the word entrepreneur would probably be a more apt description. He promised me the world, but delivered nothing.

At one stage I was supposed to be joining Austrian club Innsbruck, but that fell through at the last minute. Out of the blue

I found myself heading for Grenoble in the French first division, supposedly on a one-year deal.

I was excited. I was going to get my chance to test myself in a good league with and against top quality players. It would be strange living in a new country and dealing with the different lifestyle, but I was ready.

But my dreams of a new beginning were shattered after just four months. It had all started well enough. The pre-season was excellent and my injured knee held up very well. I played in a few friendlies and was happy with the way I played.

Sadly, the shady side of football reared its ugly head and I was involved in a very nasty situation with the player-agent-entrepreneur. This person suddenly demanded money from me for brokering the deal with Grenoble.

But my argument was simple; he had been dealing with the club and it was up to him to get his fee from them. I might have been an orphan kid but I wasn't going to be taken for a ride by this Shylock.

Suffice to say the agent never got his money but I suffered as well. I found myself back in Belgrade, disillusioned and disheartened and wondering what life would deal me next.

It didn't take me long to renew acquaintances on the café scene, more eating, drinking, talking and having fun. Yet again, this was to provide me with another opportunity and one that would ultimately change my life forever.

As luck would have it, I ran into an old friend, Tiko Jelisavcic, who I had played against. He had been an accomplished player with OFK Belgrade and Vardar Skopje. Tiko was back in Belgrade for a short break from his job as player-coach with Yugal, a Sydney club in the NSW state competition.

I showed interest in going to Australia, which was not part of FIFA at the time and Tiko, who was the Socceroos first World

Cup coach, arranged a connection with Victorian club, Footscray JUST. A deal was done and I flew to Melbourne with three other players, midfielder Veroslav Mladenovic, striker Aleksandar Jagodic, who both played with OFK and fullback Milenko Rusmir, who was a team-mate of mine at Borac.

We arrived at Essendon Airport in July 1962 to be greeted by some of the harshest weather conditions I have ever experienced. What a shock! From what I had been told, the weather in Australia was beautiful and warm and there were kangaroos everywhere.

But on this day it felt so like the Antarctic that I expected to see polar bears. It was so cold and wet and miserable and here were the four of us standing on the tarmac dressed in t-shirts and jeans. If we could have, we would have turned around, boarded that plane straight away and headed home.

We were met by a small media contingent and I remembered the funny looks on their faces when they saw how our mob was dressed. They laughed when we suggested we would only talk to them if they gave us some jumpers!

All we knew about Melbourne was that it was the capital of Victoria and that many migrant groups had established themselves there during the great migration boom of the 1950s and 1960s.

The 'ethnics' as they were known, brought a different culture with them, including their football. Many clubs were formed by these groups—Czechoslovakian, Italian, Maltese, Hungarian, Yugoslav and Greek. Footscray JUST was one of these clubs. They were formed in 1950 and in their inaugural season won the Victorian third division, going through undefeated.

But JUST was more than a football club, it was a friendly society and one which welcomed us with open arms. The club and the people involved were wonderfully generous and kind and looked after us extremely well. Nothing was a problem. We were put up in a boarding house which, coincidentally, is still standing today, in Middle Park. The only problem, however, was that the area lacked the comforts we had been used to back home.

It was a struggle to find the same type of continental food and drink we were used to and we were often forced to go to Fitzroy Street, St Kilda, to gather and eat at a place called the Spaghetti Bar which was naturally enough owned by a group of Italians. This was as close as we could get to Europe!

On the field, things were an eye-opener from the training facilities, the actual training and to the playing standard. Having been used to simply the best of everything regarding football, I likened it from going from living on the French Riviera to living in the Stone Age. The contrast was that extreme.

If we thought the facilities at our training venue, Schintler Reserve, were bad with prehistoric showers, dirty surrounds and floodlights that would have been lucky to light up an attic, then it was nothing compared to when we finally got down to some serious training.

Talk about primitive! The coach, whose name I have long forgotten, was (allegedly) an Austrian with credentials. Training was two nights a week, there was no technical training and no tactical preparation. It was simply physical fitness and running. We were training to be sprinters and marathon runners, not footballers.

Not surprisingly, Veroslav, Aleksander, Milenko and I were finding it hard to adapt to this—where else in the world would club officials form car pools to pick up players to take them to training? It did not help that we were also struggling with the culture and new lifestyle.

Of course, with no proper coaching, the team struggled badly and lost more than it won. It came as no surprise when the coach was shown the door and Jagodic took over. It was like a cultural revolution.

I had never seen such a marked change in attitude in such a short space of time. Jagodic increased training to four nights a week with a heavy emphasis on tactics, technique and preparation. Now this was more like Europe! The players could hardly believe what was happening and responded magnificently.

JUST had its own share of quality players before we arrived. There was Frank Micic, who I regarded as the most talented player in Australia at the time. He was built like German great, Franz Beckenbauer. He had speed, technique, a wonderful temperament and was a stunning shot.

Then there was Billy Rice, who played for Australia, Englishman, Cec Dickson, and a young Jim Milisavljevic, who went on to become part of the 1974 Socceroos World Cup squad. Later on, Tommy Stankovic, the man I marked in my first senior game, joined the club and went on to be regarded as one of the greatest players Australia had seen.

The players relished the new regime and that resulted in JUST playing some of the best football witnessed in Melbourne. The club won the prestigious and long-standing Docherty Cup and the Victorian State League championship in 1963.

I really enjoyed my football, though I can't say I enjoyed having to play the game at a faster pace. Australia tended to copy the British style of football which was to rush around more and get rid of the ball quickly whereas in Europe we preferred to hold the ball a bit longer and think several moves ahead.

JUST started a revolution in Victorian football. No longer was it acceptable to kick the ball downfield and run. Other clubs copied our style of football, which was to hold possession and play attractively and productively. Polonia was one club which followed us by importing top class Polish internationals in a bid to copy our style.

One of my undoubted highlights came when, along with my

three friends, I was selected in the Victorian state side to play Swiss club, FC Basel, where Socceroos Scott Chipperfield and Mile Sterjovski have been playing in more recent times.

With the likes of Stankovic, Stan Ackerley, former Polish internationals Eddie Zientara, Eddie Jankowski and Polish B international Mike Jurecki, we were outstanding, winning 3–2. I'm pleased to say I thought I had a great game and I was delighted to have made a significant contribution. I ended up playing about eight games for the state side.

Unfortunately, my stint with JUST ended after the 1964 season because of one, very important task I needed to undertake, national service duties back home. I suppose I could have put it off, even avoided it totally, but that was not in my nature. I felt I had an obligation and it was my duty to go back to join the army.

After JUST and its president, the late Tony Kovac, a renowned figure in both football and business circles in Melbourne, hosted a wonderful farewell function for me attended by 400 guests at Olympic Park, I returned to Belgrade.

When I arrived in Belgrade, I had three things on my mind, one was to complete national service, two was to complete my university degree, and three was to get a coaching degree.

From Belgrade I went to Subotica, where I had to register for duty. One of the rules of the time was that anyone doing a university degree only had to serve 11 months, instead of 18 months. I also, through some sources, knew where I was being sent for my military service.

I was to be stationed at Bileca, a little town in Herzegovina and that suited me fine. But suddenly things changed and I found myself heading south towards the Macedonian-Bulgarian border. How could this be? Something was wrong here. This was definitely not in the plan! But it did not take long to find out the reasoning behind it all.

I was mistakenly cast in the middle of a dispute I knew nothing about. It turned out that a player called Stevan Ostojic, who came from Subotica but was playing for Radnicki Nis, was being chased by two clubs—arch rivals Red Star and the army team, Partisan. He had been expected to sign with Partisan but joined Red Star at the last minute.

Ostojic was made to pay for his decision. Partisan's influence saw him being sent to the Macedonian-Bulgarian border. And I was somehow caught up in the middle of it. To this day I still don't know how it happened.

Ostojic and I quickly became known as rebels. It was unfair and I admit I was shattered and upset. Something had to be done. I got in touch with my original source who told me to jump in to a cab and go to Belgrade to meet another contact, who got me a meeting with General Ivan Gosnjak.

Incredibly, I found myself in the general's office the next day. I explained my circumstances, how I was an orphan, my football career, my trip to Australia, my university studies and the fact I was surprised to end up on the Macedonian-Bulgarian border for duty.

I must have been a good talker because the general was fantastic. He congratulated me for my honesty and contribution to the country, gave me a month's leave and told me I would be stationed at the base I was originally going to be sent to.

I eventually joined 900 recruits and was given a warm reception, being introduced to the other recruits by the general in charge as 'Rale Rasic, the footballer who has come home to do his national service'.

If I thought my status would help, I was sadly mistaken for army life was no picnic, I can assure you. The first five months were incredibly tough as they were in winter. We were often called out at one, two and three in the morning for marching and exercises. Despite this, there was always time for practical jokes like bootlaces being tied up and beds rearranged while recruits slept so that when they jumped out of bed they would bang into walls or fall over on to another bed.

Fortunately, football was never far away. Our group included the likes of Hajduk Split's Alexandar Kozlina and Andrija Ankovic and Nikola Stipic from Red Star and too many other first and second division players to name here.

Thankfully, many of the officers loved football and I had many long and entertaining discussions with them about the game. I also discovered the human side of these people, though I don't doubt that many who served in armies around the world will tell awful stories about some of those who were in charge.

My first six months went fairly quickly and I was transferred for the final five months of duty. This time, however, I was asked where I wanted to go! I chose Zrenjanin and the army base was virtually opposite the orphanage on the Begej River. I was placed in charge of a small unit.

I struck a little trouble there because the major in charge did not like football and had heard about my earlier problems. But I kept my nose clean and went by the book. It did not help the major's cause when I continually got publicity because of my connections with Zrenjanin. I suspect he did not know I was one of 'Kazalov's Babes'.

At the same time I was able to re-enrol in university while continuing my service. I passed many exams and was given 15 days off every time I passed one. Eventually I graduated as a teacher, majoring in biology and physical education.

As for coaching, I had completed all my theory work and needed only to attend three practical coaching seminars, each lasting three weeks. These seminars were brilliant because a number of the top flight coaches came from Hungary and Czechoslovakia. I graduated with honours as top of the class.

Being in Zrenjanin again was a moving experience. Every day we marched past the orphanage and every day my heart pumped faster. So many memories flooded my brain. If anyone had been looking I'm sure they would have seen the tears welling in my eyes.

It was during the many marches that I started thinking and comparing: Melbourne v Belgrade; Australia v Yugoslavia; playing v coaching; teaching v football. I was 29 going on 30. Decisions had to be made. Important decisions. Life changing decisions.

My army national service ended in July 1965. My mind was all but made up; though I decided to give playing one more go. I went to Proleter for pre-season then a month with Spartak then back to Zrenjanin.

I had been out of the game for almost a year. I was slower, misjudging headers and passes and I was caught in the Australian style of football—playing without thinking. That was it for me.

It was time to return to Melbourne and Footscray JUST.

Chapter 5

Who Would Have Thought?

I arrived back in Melbourne on January 2 1966, and a little over four years later I was coaching the Socceroos. What a transformation for me. I could hardly believe what was happening.

My life was like a tornado because things were moving so quickly. My feet never seemed to be on the ground. I was only 34 (and coaching the Socceroos) but it was like I had already crammed in 70 years of living.

While I had become obsessed by the thought of coaching, being in charge of the Australian national team had never crossed my mind. Certainly, on returning to Melbourne, my objective was to take over the reins of Footscray JUST. But I had to bide my time.

I had lost the passion for playing, but I was exceptionally fit so I played in the pre-season with the club which involved the Ampol Cup, a long-standing tournament every club wanted to win.

We made the final. After leading 3–0, we eventually held on to beat South Melbourne, one of the giants of Victorian football, 3–2. This was the moment I made my move.

During the after-match celebrations I went up to the club president, Dr Srba Preradovic, and handed him my gear—boots, tracksuit, socks and shorts—the lot. He asked, 'What's this?' I replied, 'That's the last game I play.' Well, at least I thought it would be my last game.

Not long after I was enticed to go to Sydney to play with Yugal in the NSW state competition. Yugal was a top club, but was going through some tough times even though it had 'Uncle' Joe Vlasits as coach. Joe would be appointed Socceroos coach a year (1967) later, a position he held until I replaced him in 1970.

With players like Mita Stojanovic, Ljubisa Lazarevic, Tony Ninevic, Slavko Pacanin and Joe Alagich, Yugal should have been doing a whole lot better. But for some reason, Joe was not getting the best out of them. Still, we managed to avoid relegation. I was allowed to train in Melbourne on my own and flew up to Sydney just for the games—five in all. And that was it for me as a player.

I did not miss playing, but I got a huge sense of enjoyment and satisfaction from conducting some private coaching clinics for kids in the St Kilda area because I had settled in Elwood, just south of St Kilda. I didn't know it at the time, but coaching clinics were to become a very big part of my life, even to this day.

I enjoyed it so much it was nothing for me to jump on a train, with all my gear—balls, cones, etc—and travel as far as St Albans in north-western Melbourne to do sessions with kids. And they loved it just as much as I did. It was hard work, but very satisfying. Thankfully, I have never lost that enthusiasm to impart some knowledge to the youngsters.

I estimate I have coached more than one million kids in various coaching clinics in Australia and the United States over 40 years—and enjoyed every minute of it. There is nothing like teaching kids to play football. The looks on their faces when they have learned, then mastered a skill, is something to behold.

It hasn't all been one way traffic, however, for I have got a hell of a lot out of the clinics because they have allowed me to be involved with some of the biggest names in world football who have given their time and energy to help out at various stages.

Giants of the game like Pele, Sir Stanley Matthews, Kevin Keegan, Franz Beckenbauer, Alberto Carlos, Johan Neeskens, Vladimir Bogicevic and Georgio Chinaglia were wonderful to work with. I remember during the New York Cosmos visit to Australia in 1979 we held a clinic in Adelaide which attracted 2500 kids.

In the mid-1980s, Sydney's *Sun* newspaper, through their football writer, the late David Jack, organised a series of clinics with me and Liverpool great and European footballer-of-the-year Kevin Keegan. We had more than 3000 applications and we could only take 300.

One of my most memorable moments was spending an evening with Sir Stanley Matthews in Bowral (NSW), the home of the great Sir Donald Bradman. We shared a wonderful dinner and several bottles of fine wine in front of a beautiful fire. So I got just as much from the clinics as the kids!

Probably the most successful venture was forming an Australia-wide academy with Johnny Warren during the 1970s. It was sponsored by Adidas and was a raging success.

Back in 1966 the clinics were a good way to pass time while I patiently waited for an opportunity to coach at senior level. It was also handy because it gave me time to look at various clubs and to soak in as much information on tactics, training and analysing other coaches as possible.

I didn't have to wait too long before I got—then lost—my chance to coach my beloved JUST. The club had started 1967 disastrously and they seemed headed for relegation. I was approached by the Footscray committee to take over and I agreed on one condition...I was to be sole selector.

In those days, clubs had committees to pick teams and this was often fraught with danger because committee members usually became friends with players and so this often clouded their judgment. It was a case of not what you knew but who you knew.

Footscray refused to accept my demand and that was that until the club continued to suffer from diabolical results. In the end, the committee was almost on its knees pleading with me to accept the job. And I did.

My first task was to try and change the football culture at the club and for that, I needed to win over the senior players, most of whom I had played with over the years. We were mates and close friends, but things had to change. I realised quickly that I had to go from team-mate and friend to coach and, sometimes, bastard.

I think I got my point across very strongly during the very first meeting with the senior guys. Cec Dickson, an Englishman with a bubbly personality and a great player and eventually great friend, decided to order a beer before the meeting. But I would have none of that. 'If you drink that, it will be the end of your career,' I thundered. Cec was shocked and said I was mad.

I made no apologies for my approach for I had to stamp my authority quickly and effectively. I did not mince my words with some of the players. I told them simply that not all of them would be playing regularly and that I would be using them more as substitutes when the team was in trouble. One of them was Tommy Stankovic.

Tommy was getting on in age now but he could still play in short bursts. He wasn't happy when I told him my plans for him but, later on, he would say that had I continued coaching him he would still be playing at 70!

I have to say I will never forget my debut as a coach because it was a total disaster! We were thumped 7–1 by Melbourne Hungaria. I can remember the shocked look on the faces of the committee and I knew they were asking themselves what they had got themselves into here. This looked like being a short career for me.

Fortunately, things improved. We won our next match and had

a pretty good run to finish fifth and qualify for the all-Australian play-offs.

I guess I impressed a few people with my results and methods for the next season I was also appointed coach of the Victorian state side, thanks to the help of John Barclay, who had managed Victoria when I played with them in 1962.

John offered me the coaching position, but, again, I insisted I was sole selector. There were no dramas this time. I was given total control of the state side and one of my first initiatives was to talk to some of the great footballers of the past in Victoria, guys such as Dutch international, Mike De Bruyckere, and Polish international, Vic Yancek.

I formed a five-man brains trust and told these guys the team belonged as much to them as it did to me. We worked wonderfully well as a team and I am proud to say Victoria recorded some of the greatest results in its history, including a 0–0 draw with the Greek national team and a 1–0 loss to Romania. My tenure, however, did not just involve the senior side. I now had control of all Victorian representative football from juniors to seniors.

This period of my life was like a torrent. So much was happening. I continued with my coaching clinics for the kids; I enrolled in the Toorak Teachers College; I worked as a physical education teacher at Glenroy High and Caulfield High; and married Barbara, whom I met in 1966.

Barbara gave birth to our first child, Daniela, in 1968 and I continued as coach of JUST, which was now under the control of President Tony Kovac, a larger than life figure and much respected in soccer circles in the state.

The 1968 and 1969 seasons saw Footscray emerge as one of the giants of Australian football. We won the title in 1969, the year Neil Armstrong landed on the moon.

I was fortunate in that the club had some wonderful players

who played a major role in its resurgence. Guys like Frank Micic, the superbly talented Branko Buljevic (who played for the 1974 Socceroos and was a player I regarded as one of the most gifted and respected in Australian soccer), Milan Mihajlovic, the Kazi brothers (goalkeeper Sandor and utility Andrew), Milenko Rusmir, Den Zoriaja, Milos Adamovic and goalkeeper Jimmy Milisavljevic.

After we won the title, I needed a new challenge. Much to everyone's surprise, I joined Melbourne Hungaria in 1970, the year my son, Simon, was born.

I didn't know it at the time but my move to Hungaria was probably shaped in 1966 when I met Lou Brocic. Lou had a magnificent resume, coaching Yugoslavia, Egypt and New Zealand as well as clubs such as Red Star Belgrade, Barcelona, Tenerife (Spain), Juventus (Italy) and PSV Eindhoven (Holland), where Socceroos boss Guus Hiddink is now coach.

After being brought to Australia to coach Footscray, things didn't quite work out for him and he ended up at South Melbourne, where he won the 1969 Ampol Cup but not before almost causing a riot.

Lou did a no-no during the final when he replaced revered local star, Boulis Kambouropoulos. Boulis had been with the club for 10 years and, being a Greek, he was looked on in awe. Greeks are very nationalistic and they don't like seeing their players treated in such a way. As Boulis came off the field, the fans started to throw all sorts of objects and rubbish at Lou.

It's amazing, however, how things turn out. The replacement ended up scoring the winning goal and Lou became an instant hero. One minute they were ready to lynch him, the next every Greek in Melbourne wanted to pat him on the back – and that just about sums up coaching!

Despite his standing in the game, Lou often admitted to me

that he envied how I was able to keep control of the players and rule with an iron but fair fist. He once said to me, 'I don't see this sort of control in Europe!'

My philosophy was simple I told him. 'Every club I go to, I set the rules with the players. I get their input, add some of their rules then ensure I have the final say if there are any arguments.' I have to admit that having Lou ask for coaching advice was, for me, a feather in my cap.

Lou and I were great mates and he was still coaching in his mid 80s when he passed away in Belgrade in 1995.

In the middle of 1970, I took the Victorian under 16s side to Adelaide for the national junior championships and we shocked the rest of the country by winning it. We were an eye-opener with our professionalism, training twice a day and impressing with our organisation and regimentation. Victorian officials were over the moon with the result.

No doubt I had impressed enough people in the right places for the Victorian Soccer Federation to see fit to put my name forward for the Australian senior national job. I was incredulous. So much had happened to me. Now I might get the chance to coach my adopted country. This Yugoslav with a thick accent and not very good English was now close to being a true dinky-di Aussie!

In the meantime, my career was to take yet another course. The famous Sydney club, St George Budapest, which was being coached by Frank Arok, had been aware of my growing reputation in Melbourne. Arok, who also went on to coach the Socceroos, was ready to return to Yugoslavia and suggested the club sign me as his replacement.

I flew to Sydney to watch St George, which had become known as the bridesmaids of Australian soccer because it could not win the big games that counted, play Yugal in the grand final of the NSW championship. The Saints lost 4–0 in Arok's last game in charge.

I met with the late Alex Pongrass, a giant figure in Australian football and in business. While he was a hugely successful businessman, he really didn't know much about football. I told him to leave the football to me and things would work out. We shook hands and I was now the coach of St George.

On August 13, 1970, at the age of just 34, I was appointed coach of the Socceroos. As far as I knew, the job had got down to me and Austrian Leo Baumgartner, the man they used to call the professor. He was a super player, one of the best imports to come to Australia. He had a magical career with FC Austria before coming to Australia to link with Prague. Leo and I would become huge friends in later life.

The first inkling that I had been handed the job was when John Barclay called me and said it would be nice if we could get together for a drink and a chat. He told me that he was certain the job was mine and this was confirmed several hours later when ASF secretary, Brian Le Fevre, rang.

I was the youngest coach of the national team and the first outside of NSW to be put in charge of the Socceroos. Incredibly, while I was to be full-time coach of St George, the national position was only part-time.

I was to receive the princely sum of $2000 per year—that sort of money would be lucky to pay for David Beckham's bootlace supply for a month—for two years and $3000 for the final two years—$10 000 all up.

Thankfully, money has never been an issue with me. I was excited by the challenge and I would have coached the Socceroos for nothing.

Of course, these days it is a different story. Look at England's Sven-Goran Eriksson. The man who will replace him after the 2006 World Cup finals will, reportedly, be offered $10 million per year.

Chapter 6

Start of the Long Road

Soon after my appointment I flew to Sydney where I met the then Australian Soccer Federation president Arthur George (he was a Sir at the time after being knighted but I refuse to use the title in this book for reasons I prefer to keep to myself) at the federation's offices in Clarence Street. We got on quite well at that stage, but little did I know that things would turn so sour a little under four years later.

I was well prepared for the meeting with the most powerful man in the sport in the country. I had big plans and, as usual, I wasn't going to compromise on anything. For me, it was all about the squad and giving it the best possible chance to succeed. There would be no short cuts, no skimping and no excuses. It was my way or forget it.

As far as I was concerned, I had my four-year plan, which no other coach of the national team had had the courage or knowledge to put in front of people like Arthur George.

While I had never met Arthur, I was expecting some strong opposition to my demands. I had already learned that side of the football culture in Australia from picking teams to running the finances, Australian soccer officials at all levels didn't like to give away control. I didn't expect him to be any different, though it should be remembered that he was also new on the starting block in these sorts of matters which obviously made it easier for me.

As it turned out, he was a pushover at the start. I gave him my blueprint, which included a six-week world tour stretching from New Caledonia to Asia to Europe then Mexico. It wasn't going to be cheap nor would the lead-up to the trip be cheap. I was going for broke.

I started with a week-long camp at the Fox and Hound Motel in Wahroonga (Sydney), which would become a regular home base for the squad and would be the setting for some great stories, incidents and funny moments.

One particularly funny incident will stay with me forever and involved former *Sydney Morning Herald* soccer writer, Brian Mossop, a kind, gentle man whom I took a great liking to. Brian was not your typical, hard-nosed journalist. He hated offending people and preferred to nurture friendships among the people he wrote about.

On this occasion Brian, uncharacteristically, had written something that Max Tolson and a few of the Socceroos took exception to. He turned up at Wahroonga to do an interview with me a few days after the story appeared, immaculately dressed, as usual, wearing a splendid blue suit and matching tie.

It was a bloody cold winter's day in June and Brian, who was completely unaware of the problems he had caused with the players, had to walk past the hotel swimming pool to get to me. But he was intercepted by Tolson, who put his arm around him and said, 'Hello mate, great to see you.'

Brian's face lit up and he felt delighted with the warm greeting. 'That's a lovely watch you are wearing Brian, can I have a look at it?" Max asked. Brian handed over the watch. 'How much money have you got in your wallet, mate?' Max asked. The still unsuspecting Mossop laughed, took out his wallet and started counting the money.

That was the signal. Suddenly Max grabbed him and a few of the Socceroos rushed over as well and Brian ended up in the pool. The water was so cold and the poor man was shivering. Through chattering teeth, and a smile, he simply said, 'You bastards!'

We got Brian changed into an Australian tracksuit and invited him to stay for lunch. In the meantime, the hotel owner had taken his lovely suit and put it in the dryer. And you know what's coming next. The jacket sleeves had shrunk to just below his elbows and the pants only came down to just below his knees. It brought more uproar from the Socceroos and Brian laughed his head off as well.

The Wahroonga base was going to set the tone for the next three to four years and I wanted everything to be precise, almost perfect.

Two months before the camp I decided to check out the hotel and met with the owners, Ashley and Linda Gerald. To say we did not hit it off immediately is an understatement. They were not prepared for Cyclone Rale!

Among a long list of demands, I wanted rooms at the back of the complex to avoid the noise from the Pacific Highway and the players, as many as 26, had to have three meals a day—all cooked.

Previous Australian teams were more used to sandwiches, fruit, coffee and tea. It was simple stuff, but no way to treat semi-professional footballers who were about to embark on a fully professional training environment.

I could see Ashley was aghast. 'And who the fuck is going to pay for all of this?' he asked incredulously. I wasn't used to this sort of response. I simply scribbled down Arthur's phone number and told Ashley to speak to him.

Arthur's response was, 'Just give him what he wants. He is a tough bastard. We will fix up the bill.' Arthur had barely known me two months but he was already used to me.

But if Ashley thought that was the end of it, he was wrong. I demanded a meeting with the chef and his staff. The chef barely had time to say hello before I put my demands on him. 'I want long plates, not round. I want good, quality food. I want it hot.

'I want the biggest, thickest and best steaks you can buy. I want the steak to be so big it hangs over the plate and I want it cooked rare and with the blood oozing out. I want the butt of beef served whole so that the players can cut off their own piece of steak.' There was method to my madness though I could understand that Ashley, Linda and the chef could not see it for the life of them!

On the first day of the camp the players were astounded. I could see their eyes popping out of their heads. Don't forget, they were mainly part-time footballers—semi-professionals. They had jobs, many of them were not that well off and they had not seen anything like this.

The steaks were an instant winner. At our first official team meeting after dinner, I asked the players what they thought of the steaks. In a virtual chorus they sang back 'fucking beautiful' though a few complained there was too much blood. 'Get used to it,' I said. 'That's what I expect from you for the next four years.' The tone had been set.

As in all the clubs I had been involved in as a coach, the next task was to lay down the rules. I handed them out to the players along with a blank piece of paper so that they could put down their own rules. I combined some of them with mine and that was that. The players signed the rules and, from then on, there were never any major problems.

While everything was five-star off the field, the players never forgot what they were in camp for. They worked their bums off three times a day, every day. This comprised of a long run before breakfast, an 11.30am session then a 4pm session. All sessions were held at the well appointed Engelfield Stadium in Dural.

Englefield Stadium, which was the dream of former cricketer and property developer, Bill Englefield, was supposed to be the state-of-the-art sporting complex of the day. However, the players did not think too kindly of it at times, especially when it rained and churned up the chicken manure that was often used to fertilise the field. The smell usually lasted weeks.

The routine was part of the mental conditioning I had planned for the players. My thinking was influenced by my experience in Europe, especially with the Eastern bloc countries like Hungary, Yugoslavia, East Germany, Poland, Russia and Czechoslovakia.

The players said it was the best week they had ever had as footballers. But then I had to make the tough decisions. I had to choose my first squad for the world tour. Of course, there were problems. A number of players simply couldn't get the time off work. They were not allowed to take leave. That's the way it was in those days though I'm positive had they been rugby league players or cricketers they would not have had the same dramas. 'Wog ball' wasn't on the Australian sporting radar, so no-one cared.

John Watkiss, Ray Baartz, Alan Marnoch and Atti Abonyi couldn't go because of work commitments. I selected a mixture of players, throwing in veterans like John Warren, Billy Vojtek and Manfred Schaefer with the likes of Jack Reilly, George Blues, Dennis Yaager, Mike Denton, John Roche, John Doyle, John Perin, Sandy Irvine, Col Curran, Jimmy Mackay and Peter Wilson, who were all making their international debuts. Ray Richards and Adrian Alston, who were not yet established players, were to make a mark on the tour.

The tour was an unusual thing for me. As a club coach, winning was everything. You lived and died by it. Lose too many games and the committee would sack you. There was always pressure to succeed. And I thrived on it. But the Socceroos job, at this stage anyway, was something different.

I had a four-year plan that would lead to a specific ending. It was a carefully thought out and calculated plan. The world tour was a small, but significant stage of the plan. Therefore, winning wasn't everything. It was much more important to build mateship, to re-establish veteran players, establish those on the fringe and discover new talent. If we won games, fine. If we lost, well, we could cope as long as we showed something for it.

As well, I wasn't necessarily looking for gifted players, but more for the strong characters—those with mental toughness who would never give up, who would run through a brick wall and who would bleed for their mates and their country.

There was another important aspect I tried to build in to the players and that was that as far as I was concerned, all that counted was the first XI. It didn't matter in what situation – training, friendly or serious matches. I made it clear to the players that they should never want to be numbers 12, 13, 14, 15 and so on. I wanted them to strive to get in to the best XI at all times.

This meant that there were times when I was questioned about my methods. I remember one journalist asked me whether the players thought I was too brutal at times. I replied, 'Not at times, but always when there was a question of commitment to the team and Australian soccer.'

I made that my philosophy for my entire career as a coach. Discipline for all was the only way to go as far as I was concerned.

We headed off to New Caledonia in October 1970, where we beat the home side 3–1 and 1–0 before beating the Jardine Sports Club 3–0 in Hong Kong. A 9–0 thrashing of Macau, thanks to a hat-trick from Mike Denton, really had us in high spirits. But I was quick to warn the players not to get carried away because of the weak opposition.

After a 0–0 draw with Ogheb in Iran we met the national team in Tehran on November 4, producing a wonderful 2–1 win. Three years later we would find ourselves in the same environment but at a different venue against an Iranian side playing like a team of supermen and high on the support of a wildly fanatical crowd in what was to be a defining moment for Australian soccer.

The 1970 match against Iran was a super result as I fielded only three players—Schaefer, Warren and Vojtek—who had more than 20 caps apiece. Eight players—Reilly, Roche, Denton, Yaager, Blues, Curran, Mackay and Wilson—made their A-international debuts.

It was in Tehran that I encountered my first problem with player discipline. I had warned the players that the team curfew had to be strictly observed, yet Dave Keddie and John Doyle chose to ignore it. Assistant coach Les Scheinflug and I had decided to do the rounds of the rooms at around 10pm delivering bottles of Coke as a pretence to check on them.

When we got to Keddie's and Doyle's room I noticed that John, who was lying down on his bed with blankets partially over him, was wearing socks. When we walked out I said to Les, 'these bastards are up to something' and that he should go downstairs and wait. The players had forgotten that I had not been long retired as a player, so I knew every trick in the book.

About 30 minutes later, Les sprung them as they were about to walk out of the hotel. It had been previously reported that I had been hiding behind a sofa waiting to see if anyone had broken the curfew, but I am innocent. It was Les who had been waiting ever so patiently.

After a 3–3 draw with a Tehran XI, we travelled to Israel and beat club side Hapoel 2–1 in Haifa in a warm-up to an international against the highly fancied Israeli national team on November 10.

Israel had a very good squad and was still on a high after some superb performances at the World Cup finals in Mexico where they lost 2–0 to Uruguay before drawing 1–1 with Sweden and 0–0 with Italy. Israel finished bottom of their group on two points but were just two points from group winners Italy and a point behind second-placed Uruguay.

Not surprisingly, the Socceroos were not expected to get close to the Israelis, but a stunning 51st minute goal from Ray Richards gave us an amazing 1–0 win—a victory that not only rocked Israeli football but caused people back home to sit up and take notice.

Not long after, we landed in Athens for a match against the powerful Greek national team on November 17. Again, we were the huge underdogs. Even a draw would be a shock result for the Greeks had not lost at home for many, many years.

To that end, I pushed the players even harder. Despite having already been on the road for some time and played so many matches, I had them training twice a day. A good result against the Greeks would be a huge feather in the caps of the players.

Interestingly, the great Hungarian master, Ferenc Puskas, who was coaching Panathinaikos at the time and went on to coach South Melbourne in the National Soccer League for several seasons in the 1980s, was an observer at one of our training sessions.

He was taken aback by my training regimen for the players and asked our physiotherapist, Peter Van Ryn, why we would train so hard a day before the match.

The answer was there for all to see the next day. Goals from Mackay, Alston and Blues gave the Socceroos an upset 3–1 win over the Greeks, who were subsequently fined $150 each as a result. At the end of the game, Peter spotted Puskas, raced over to him and said simply, 'Coach [Rale] crazy, huh!' Puskas, in awe, replied, 'No, no.'

That match will long live in my memory. It was a truly remarkable achievement. The players were outstanding. Everyone did his job. It was almost the perfect game for us. I know the victory caused a scene back home, especially in Melbourne among the huge Greek community. It also made big news in Europe.

I also remember the game because it was the first time I clashed with John Warren. At half-time I saw John sitting in the corner of the dressing room and he was quite agitated, swearing profusely and with a sour look on his face.

I approached him and said, 'Excuse me John, what is [the word] fuck about?'

He replied, 'No-one is marking out there.' At this stage I was very annoyed. 'I can't see any problems with the other players. Jimmy Mackay has marked [Greek legend] Mimis Domazos out of the game and Richards has done the same with [Dimitris] Papaioannou. 'The only problem I see is that the man you are marking [Kostas Eleftherakis] scored the goal. He is your opponent. I give you 10 minutes to sort it out or else.'

Well John was like a bull to a red rag. He charged at the door, bashed it open then went out and demolished Eleftherakis. That, however, wasn't the end of it. After the match I went over to John, who was also captain of the St George side I was coaching, to congratulate him on his fine second half. I said to him, 'Well done. I should criticise you more often!' as I put my hand on his head.

But he reacted negatively and said something I didn't quite pick up. It sounded like he said 'no-one tells me what to do'. I opted to give him the benefit of the doubt—until we got back to the hotel.

When we arrived at the hotel, we were greeted by some of the most amazing scenes I have ever witnessed. There were literally hundreds of photographers waiting for us. The players were stunned. They couldn't believe their eyes.

As soon as we walked into the foyer, I summoned John to my room. I told him that the captain was also a coach on the field, but the team can have only one boss and that was me. I have always believed that it is no use playing hard with players who are well below the borderline in terms of ability. But you always ask the maximum from your top-line players because you know they can deliver. John fell into the latter category.

'Let's get straight to the point, John,' I said. 'It is either my way or no way at all. I'll give you five minutes to think about it.' I then held my breath. To be honest, I don't think John had ever been spoken to or challenged in such a way before. I didn't know what to expect from him or how he would react. He was a passionate man about his football and would allow nothing to get in his way.

John didn't need all the five minutes to come back with his answer. 'It's your way, Rale'. Later in his biography, *Poofters, Wogs and Sheilas*, John described the 1974 Socceroos as 'Rale's team'.

After the Israel result, I was starting to think I had something special here. Now I was just about convinced.

It was at an official reception hosted by the Greek federation at the Acropolis after the game that I first started to wonder about Australian soccer officialdom. The Greek minister for sport spoke immaculately and praised the Socceroos before the president of the Greek federation presented our tour leader, Ian Brusasco, with a magnificent statue as a gift.

Brusasco, who is a prominent Queensland businessman and succeeded Arthur George as president of the ASF in the late 1980s, responded without a hint of humour, 'This is fantastic but how do we carry this back home?' I thought this was humiliating and showed a lack of class and diplomacy.

But I rectified the situation by getting up to speak after Brusasco and complimented the Greeks for the privilege of playing against them, their contribution to football and their magnificent contribution to the world through centuries of history. The Greek officials were simply amazed by my speech and applauded wildly. They appreciated it so much. A little goodwill goes a long way.

A few days later we drew 1–1 with the Greek under 23 side in Kavala before heading to England for the final leg of the European tour.

We were stationed in London and I would have face-to-face dramas with Brusasco. But first we beat the Harry Haslem-coached Luton Town 2–1 in absolutely atrocious conditions—ankle deep mud, rain and freezing cold. Still, it was a terrific effort by the boys against a side that included the likes of Malcom MacDonald (Supermac) and Mike Keen. Coincidentally, Adrian Alston, who was on the tour, played with Luton later in his career.

It was in Luton that some of the players were given an awful fright one night. Alston was showing some of the players a few sights in the area when he pointed to a far paddock where two girls had been murdered years earlier. It was said that when there was a full moon the girls would appear.

This night the boys saw a figure, distinguished by white teeth. For once, Alston, the joker of the squad, was speechless. But as the figure drew closer, the nerves eased. It was Harry Williams, the only Aborigine in the squad. Harry had a great laugh when told why the players were so quiet and looking very pale.

Harry is a great guy with a terrific sense of humour. He was always easy going even though he was on the end of light-hearted comments from team-mates such as, 'Come out of the shadows, we can't see you' and 'if you don't watch it, we will give you a white eye'. They were different days I guess and I suppose things like that would not do in these days of political correctness.

Next up we were due to play what I thought would be a full strength Manchester City at Maine Road. But the day before the game, I saw a headline in the local newspaper that read 'Manchester Babies to play undefeated Aussies'. City would be fielding a virtual reserves team.

I stormed into Brusasco's room and showed him the newspaper. 'So what,' he said. 'We are only here for the money.' I was infuriated. We were being treated like second-rate citizens. It wasn't good enough.

As an international team we deserved to be treated with more respect. I know that Australian sides were forced to play against club sides a lot in the late 1970s and in the 1980s but, thankfully, it doesn't happen any more.

Anyway, we lost the match 2–0—our first defeat—and I was furious. The next day the newspaper heading read, 'Stick to cricket!' My blood was really boiling now. Again, I took the newspaper to Brusasco's room and again I got the cold shoulder. By this time our relationship was in tatters. I got on far better with the other tour leader, Frank Parsons, who was a kind and educated person. Frank often sided with me privately but he was number two and did not want to cause problems with Brusasco.

Another loss, 1–0 to an Irish representative team, followed as I took a reduced squad to Ireland while other members stayed in London under the care of Scheinflug.

It was in Dublin where I experienced one of the very few problems I had dealing with players. Billy Vojtek was an extremely gifted player who had become well established in the Socceroos squad under previous coach Joe Vlasits. We were both heavily involved in Victorian soccer so I knew him pretty well.

I did not select him in the starting line-up against Ireland but intended using him for the second half. I did not notice that he was not getting changed into his gear in the dressing room before the game until Peter Van Ryn whispered it to me.

Apparently, Billy considered he had been playing well enough to be picked to start the game. It did not help that several teammates had been winding him up in the hotel and telling him he was right and that he should be starting. Well Billy elected not to bring his boots to the ground.

I was furious. I shouted at him to get out of the room and Billy left immediately. He ended up watching the game from the grandstand.

In later years he told a journalist, the late Laurie Schwab, he was so ashamed of what he did and having to face the other players and had almost decided to walk back to the hotel instead of watching the game. He also admitted I had every right to do what I did both in team selections and ordering him out of the room.

Billy was subsequently suspended from the last match against Mexico and fined a week's wages. A few days later, Lou Gautier wrote in *Soccer World* magazine in Sydney that Vojtek had declared he would never play for Australia again. When we returned from the tour, Billy and I had a discussion. I told him I did not recognise reputations and anyone who is not prepared to work for the team.

Despite all of that, I gave him an opportunity in three matches against Israel in 1971 but as far as I was concerned, the damage had already been done. For me it was irreparable. He wasn't the strong, committed, loyal character I was looking for. It cost him dearly in the end.

Talk about football paradise. Mexico had just hosted the World Cup and the country was still on a huge high. The match against the Mexicans was always going to be a huge assignment. The players struggled in the conditions. They were not used to the lack of oxygen at high altitude. A 3–0 loss probably wasn't too bad under the circumstances.

Our Mexican hotel, which was also the headquarters of the Mexican Football Federation, was the scene of some of the more hilarious practical jokes played on the tour by the players. It was the end of the tour and the players had so much free time on their hands.

Some of the players quickly realised there was fun to be had by tipping buckets of water from the seventh floor onto unsuspecting victims, usually team-mates or officials, below as they entered the hotel. One victim was the squad doctor, Brian Corrigan.

One day an immaculately dressed Corrigan had spent half an hour getting his hair done in the hotel barber shop before attending an important meeting. No sooner had he walked out of the hotel than a bucket of cold water tumbled down on him. To his great credit, Brian simply stood there, parted his hair, looked up and smiled, calling out 'you bastards' before returning to his room to get changed.

But the players walked a thin line when a local businessman in a very expensive suit and his lady copped the same treatment. Both he and his very attractive companion stormed into the lobby shouting abuse and threatening to sue those responsible. To this day we still don't know who was responsible, though the usual suspects such as Curran, Richards, Wilson, Warren and Schaefer were high on the list.

For some reason Corrigan was usually the target of many of the practical jokes. On the second last evening of the tour in Mexico, he went out and while he was gone, Schaefer, Richards, Wilson and Warren stripped his room bare. There was not a single piece of furniture left once they had finished. Everything had been stacked in the rooms of the players.

When the doctor returned and discovered what had happened, he knocked on my door and he said, 'Where do you think I am going to sleep' before telling me what had happened. He ended up sleeping in team official Tom Patrick's room.

Again, for some strange reason, players Jimmy Mackay and Sandy Irvine were spared from the jokes by their team-mates—until one day on the Mexican tour. Jimmy and Sandy were always wondering why their room had never been done over. This day, they were getting ready to go out on the town. They were happy and singing.

As most Scotsmen do, they put on their socks, shirts then underpants last before putting on their trousers and shoes. Jimmy, however, was in for a shock. As he put his foot in his shoe, he let out a scream, shouting 'fucking bastards'. Someone had filled the toe of his shoe, which had been left out on the balcony, with thick, black shoe polish. As Jimmy put his foot in, the polish, which had become soft and almost liquid like due to the intense outside heat, squirted out all over the place. Jimmy was angry that he had to go out and buy a brand new pair of shoes.

Despite the loss to Mexico, we returned to Australia to a very positive response from the fans and especially the media. The tour had been an incredible success. I had learned so much, as did the players. The officials? Well, maybe not so much.

For me, the World Cup ball was rolling...and quickly.

Chapter 7

Warren, Wilson and the Socceroos Captaincy

Peter Wilson and John Warren are two of the greatest symbols the game in this country has produced and I had the pleasure of coaching both of them.

Unfortunately, I had more to do with John when he was nearer the end of his career while, over the years, I have been asked more questions about Peter Wilson than any other player I have ever been involved with.

There is no doubt in my mind that John and Peter had an aura about them, a presence, something that stood them apart from the rest. They defined the great Australian sportsman—fit, strong-willed, determined and afraid of nothing.

But my goodness, you could not meet two more different personalities, two more complex characters. I've always said if we could have combined the two personalities and playing abilities we would have had the greatest Australian captain of all time!

Charisma is sometimes used to describe sports people. John Warren had it by the bucket full. He was always about making a good impression. It was important for John to be looked on as a good guy, which, basically, he was.

On the other hand, Peter never knew how to spell the word charisma and never cared much about what people thought about him.

John's biggest asset was his personality. He was always polite and charming, greeting people with that infectious smile of his. He was particularly terrific with people he would meet for the first time and would speak to them as though he had known them for years.

It was little wonder that he became a darling of the journalists and radio and television reporters and eventually found himself a huge part of the media both during and after his playing days. John and the media were made for each other. A marriage made in football heaven.

John used the media to his greatest advantage, not on a personal basis but for the good of the game. Football was his dream, his immeasurable passion. He was forever trying to portray it in a good light. By the same token, the game was good to him in return, helping him build his image and businesses. I first met John in 1968 when Australia played against Greece then again when he played for NSW against Victoria when Josef Venglos (who went on to coach Czechoslovakia, Austria, Scottish giants Celtic and Aston Villa in the premier league) was coach. You could see he was a special player.

He had speed and incredible acceleration, good technique and superb fighting qualities. He was also a deadly finisher in front of goal and determined to the extreme. If John, who was so widely respected by the players, had a fault it was that he was a little unpredictable and moody at times.

When I took over as Socceroos coach in 1970, John was captain and had been part of the national team since 1966. He retained the captaincy under me. Indeed, up until an awful injury in 1971 that almost ended his career it would have been unthinkable that he would not be captain of the national team.

The fact that John recovered from a cruciate ligament injury that ended the careers of 99 per cent of the players who suffered such an injury in those days, is testament to his strong will and fighting instincts. To be honest, I never thought he would recover from that crushing blow—and a lesser man would not have.

If ever there was a more stark contrast to John Warren in terms of personality, it was Peter Wilson. Off the field, Peter was an introverted, shy type of person who had a heart of gold.

He was an honest man who said what he thought. But he was not as good with the public or the media as John, though many journalists held Peter in awe. Peter was happiest when he was around football and his team-mates.

Peter, however, had an incredibly dry sense of humour and liked to play practical jokes. The *Daily Telegraph's* John Taylor told me of the time he toured with Peter and the Socceroos in the late 1970s when he was just starting off as a soccer writer. Peter had somehow got hold of some sawdust and had placed it in John's luggage.

When John unpacked his bag in the hotel, all his clothes were covered in sawdust. John subsequently found out Peter was responsible and plotted to get his revenge. It came at breakfast a couple of mornings later.

Peter usually sat in the same place in the restaurant. He got himself a cup of tea, placed it on his table then went to get some food. In the meantime, John had unscrewed a salt container and poured the entire contents into Peter's cup of tea.

John said the players saw what he was doing and couldn't believe their eyes. They were certain Peter would blow up in a rage and they warned John not to do it.

When Peter finally took a sip of his tea, he spat it all over the place. John said the look on his face was incredible, but that Peter took it in the right spirit. From then on Peter left John alone.

Peter usually had the players in fits of laughter and he was great to have around on tours and in camps. I remember one time Peter had to get up to respond to a speech at a function after a match in Tel Aviv on one of our overseas tours. He hated doing those things so we did not know what to expect when he got up.

The speech was short and simple and went something like this, 'Thank you. I'd just like to thank the person who invented the Venetian blinds. If it wasn't for him, it would be curtains for us.' He then returned to his seat as the entire squad broke up in fits of laughter. It was a real shame that those outside of his comfortable environment never got to experience that side of him.

On the field Peter, who was known as Willy to his team-mates, though I always called him Peter, was the absolute boss—a towering, imposing figure who could do as much damage with just one, icy stare as he could with his overwhelming physical presence.

He was so powerful and strong, and commanded his area of the field like a pack of hungry dogs. Peter was very good in the air and could read a game superbly.

I had a special relationship with him because I felt he understood how I thought about football. We were usually on the same wavelength and it was like having an extra coach out on the field. I would only have to look at Peter or make a slight hand movement during a game and he would know instantly what I wanted.

Peter and I often spent hours and hours talking about the game, tactics and especially the needs of the players. He had a vast knowledge of a lot of things to do with football.

When I gave him the captaincy while John was injured he slipped into the role like he was born to it. He was a leader in every sense and the players thought the world of him. You could see they would run through a brick wall if he asked them.

With John not playing and looking like he would not come

back, the thought of having to make a choice for the Socceroos captaincy never really crossed my mind. As I said, no one really gave John a chance of recovering from the injury.

But as champions prove so often, John did make it back and I was left with a decision that understandably sparked huge debate in the media (a number of journalists were siding with John) and soccer circles at the time.

To be honest, it was a tough time for me, as there was almost intolerable pressure from the Australian Soccer Federation and the media to make a decision. Australians, more so than any other people around the world, seem to have a fixation with captains no matter what sport and no matter whether it be at club or national team level. They quickly put these men and women on a pedestal and they are treated almost like gods and, at the same time, put under enormous strain.

That is why there are few more coveted privileges in Australian sport than to captain your nation, whether it is cricket, rugby league, rugby union, soccer or any other code. When Australian sporting teams win or lose, there is usually tremendous focus on the captain.

Many can handle the job, some can't. I'll always remember that fine cricketer, Kim Hughes, breaking down and crying at a press conference in which he announced he was standing down as captain of the Australian cricket side. He was making a statement and couldn't finish it. That's what the captaincy, or losing it, can do to a person.

I knew at the time just how much the captaincy meant to John. He gave a clue just how much in his marvellous 2002 book *Sheilas, Wogs and Poofters* when he wrote, 'having to watch someone else lead out the team when Australia played was worse than I had ever imagined. As captain, I felt it had been my team and now someone else had taken my place.'

I know John expected to be given back the captaincy once he had shown he was still capable of playing for the national team. He wrote, 'Even now I feel I should have been captain, so it is something that I look back on with a great deal of disappointment and regret.

'I somehow expected to be treated with a little special consideration because of my record. But the whole Socceroos set-up had changed while I was out. When I returned, I discovered the Socceroos clearly wasn't my team any more and had very much become the domain of new coach Rale Rasic.'

Things were never really the same between John and me after that, something John freely admitted in his book, and we had our share of arguments.

It was a strange feeling fighting with Johnny because I was always close to his parents, his late father, Victor, and his mother, Marj. She treated me like one of her own sons. She used to ring me up every now and then when she got wind that John and I were fighting. She'd say, 'Rale, is everything okay with you and John? If it isn't fix it. I love you both.' She is a truly remarkable lady and will always be in my heart.

To be honest, choosing between Peter and John wasn't a hard decision for me to make. In the end, it came down to the fact that Peter had become so well established in the side. He had created this wonderful, powerful image in the defence and there is no doubt the players looked up to him and were inspired by him.

John, on the other hand, was not the same player as he was before the injury. That was clear to everyone and I think he admitted that. So he was not guaranteed a spot in the starting line-up and I wasn't about to give the captaincy to him under those circumstances.

As it was, John played in the first World Cup qualifying game against South Korea but took no part in the second leg or in the final match in Hong Kong when we finally qualified for the finals.

I remember telling John that Peter would remain captain and he was naturally disappointed. It was obvious he was hurting, but he told me he understood the situation.

John was to be the vice-captain of the team, but I can reveal now, for the first time, that had Ray Baartz gone to Germany as a player, he would have been vice-captain and not John Warren.

Having given John the news, I was quick to assure him that there was no way he would miss out on going to the World Cup finals, though there were no guarantees of a starting spot. John ended up playing in the opening game against East Germany, but didn't start in the other two matches against West Germany and Chile.

If ever a man deserved to be in that squad it was John Warren. This was a reward for his incredible contribution to the game, for his undeniable passion and dedication and for his amazing fight-back from an injury that would have destroyed a lesser person.

John and Peter took remarkably different paths once they had finished with the playing side of the game. John threw himself totally into the sport through the media, coaching, junior clinics, administration and marketing. It was his life.

He lived and breathed the game every minute of the day. It consumed him. Just in his playing days, John had become the face of Australian soccer. He was a revered figure, an icon. He worked tirelessly through the media, television, radio and newspapers, to push the game beyond the boundaries.

When he died of cancer in 2004, our game lost its hero, its champion, its heart and soul. There was emptiness in the game and many wondered where the inspiration would come from to continue his wonderful work.

But as it has shown over the years, Australian soccer is a resilient beast. The game is enjoying a renaissance at club level through the A-League and the icing on the cake was that wonderful and extraordinary moment on November 16 2005 when John Aloisi scored in the penalty shoot-out to take Australia to the World Cup finals for the first time since 1974. You could almost feel John's presence that night in the stands, among his people, the fans, the believers. Peter was a different story. He went the opposite way to John. He continued captaining and playing for the Socceroos and various clubs for the next three or four years before being lost to the game forever.

In what was a sad indictment of our game, Peter quit in disillusionment after being let down twice by officialdom. The first time was over bonus payments from the ASF for the World Cup finals. He was totally disillusioned because the ASF would not release the official monetary figures for qualifying for Germany. Even to this day no one knows how much money the ASF received. You would have to suspect, however, that the players may not have received an appropiate share.

It all became too much for Peter in the early 1980s when a certain club official made promises regarding bonuses for Apia winning the NSL Cup but failed to deliver. Peter was playing and coaching one day, then gone the next. It was as if he had disappeared from the face of the earth.

He closeted himself away in Wollongong, where he worked in the mines and wanted nothing more to do with the game. I know numerous journalists, including some who knew him well, tried countless times to get him to tell his story. But it was a waste of time.

Peter is a proud, quiet man who does not like being made a fuss of. He is happiest when he can live on acreage, look after a few animals and muck around with his Harley Davidson motorbikes. He simply doesn't need or want the media attention. He just wants to be left in peace.

That's why I, along with a great number of the 1974 Socceroos, was hugely disappointed when the media finally tracked him down at his property on the South Coast several weeks before Australia was due to play Uruguay in the World Cup qualifiers in 2005.

The newspaper had its journalist and a photographer camp outside his property for several days. When Peter came out to feed his animals, they took photos of him that did not portray him in the best light.

He refused to talk to the journalist but it did not stop the newspaper from printing a huge article. I just don't know why they did not leave him alone and respect his request for privacy.

As a result of that story, Peter has again been forced to move house to avoid being pestered by the media. After what he did for the game in this country, he deserves his peace and quiet and to be left alone. The journalist should be embarrassed by what he did to Peter.

Sadly, to this day, and despite numerous attempts, Peter also refuses to attend Socceroos reunions. He told me once that he just wouldn't be able to handle all the fuss. Some of the 1974 Socceroos like Adrian Alston and Jim Fraser still maintain reasonable contact with him.

There is one man, the remarkable and some say eccentric Andre Krueger—a resident of Hanover in Germany—who has probably had more contact with him over the past five or six years than anyone else. Andre and I have become friends over the past eight years or so through his fascination with the Socceroos, especially the 1974 squad.

He has made special trips to Australia, paying out of his own pocket, to attend various functions over the years and has assembled a remarkable memorabilia collection. Of course, my collection is much better than his and I love it when he comes to Australia and visits me at home!

Andre, who proudly calls himself 'zeh crazy German', spends hours in my soccer museum, taking photographs and drooling over the memorabilia. I have given him little bits and pieces over the years but the thing he covets most is a pair of Peter's boots, the ones he gave away after the World Cup finals, which I have in my possession.

Andre has become somewhat of a celebrity in this country and back home in Hanover. On his trips here for the last two World Cup qualifying campaigns (2001 and 2005), he was given massive publicity by the media, featuring in a number of newspaper articles, on television and on the radio because of his love of all things Socceroos, but especially the 1974 squad.

I know Andre, who has dedicated a website (The Southern Cross) to the Soccceroos and Peter has spoken a number of times on the telephone to him and has visited him several times at his property.

Andre tells a fantastic story about the first time he met Peter in person when he was playing in a national league match for South Coast United in the late 1970s. Andre's passion for the 1974 Socceroos developed when he was about 12. Though he did not get to see us play live in the World Cup finals, he followed our results religiously and Peter became his favourite Australian player.

When he was in his late teens, Andre got a job on a ship as a merchant seaman and when the ship was heading to Sydney, he saw it as his chance to track down Wilson.

Once he got to Sydney, he had a few days off. He found out Peter would be playing at Englefield Stadium so he jumped in a taxi and asked to be taken there. Andre suspected something was wrong when the driver pulled up in the centre of a suburb and there were no football grounds in sight. The driver had stopped in Enfield.

He radioed the base and discovered Andre needed to be at Englefield Stadium in Dural—a long, long way from Enfield. 'Zeh crazy German' still wanted the driver to take him there because he thought it couldn't be that far away. The driver did the right thing by him and dropped him off at the nearest railway station.

Andre finally got to the ground, watched Peter play then told an official about his long, long trip and the reason for it. He was taken into the dressing room and Peter, who was absolutely stunned by it all, welcomed him with open arms. Andre said they spoke for ages.

All I can say is that Andre is a very privileged man to have the tremendous access these days to one of the true icons of the local game.

Maybe one day Peter will come to one of our re-unions because, despite his long absence, he will always be part of our very, very special family and will always be welcome.

Chapter 8

Club, Controversy, Socceroos and More Controversy

I was still on a high when I returned from the world tour to Sydney to take up my duties with St George, but it was to be a short and tempestuous combination. It should have been the marriage made in heaven and, for a while, it was.

To his credit, Frank Arok had been the catalyst for great change at the club and in Australian soccer in general. He was a visionary, a football intellect. Yes, he was a bit of an extrovert, even a showman and his methods were, at times, unconventional (something he maintained throughout his coaching career in Australia). The game here had not seen anything like him yet it embraced him warmly.

Arok, who had won over players, officials and the media with his outgoing nature and knowledge of the game, operated more like a European coach, introducing daily afternoon training sessions, all sorts of specialised equipment and a fulltime gear steward. Everything was located at the team's training headquarters at Barton Park.

When I took over from him, everything was in place. I could not have asked for more. My job was to enhance the situation. But there was one big change that was needed. Despite its exalted stature, the club had become known as the bridesmaid of Australian soccer.

My goal was to take St George to the 1971 championship, but first there was the question of the Tokyo International Cup—a tournament organised by St George president, Alex Pongrass, renowned soccer journalist, Andrew Dettre, and Japanese Football Association president, Sun-ichiro Okano.

We competed against three other teams, the Japanese national side, their B side and Danish division one club Boldklubben Frem. It was going to be formidable opposition and I have no doubt there were many sceptics laughing off our chances when we left for Tokyo.

St George played two warm-up matches en-route to Japan, beating Macau 6–0 and Hong Kong's Jardine Sports Club also 6–0. Two warm-up games in Tokyo also resulted in a 3–2 win over Toyo Kogyo in Hiroshima and 2–1 against Hitachi FC in Ominya. The boys were full of confidence by the time we came up against the Japanese B team.

The team played out of its skin. The Japanese did not know what hit them. We were too fast, too strong and too fit for them and the 6–2 final scoreline flattered them to say the least. In our next game we drew 0–0 with the full Japanese national team and that really set us up nicely for the tournament

In the final match, we outclassed the Danes 3–0. Players such as Adrian Alston, John Warren, Harry Williams, Alan Ainslie, Mike Denton and Doug Utjesenovic were outstanding. It was good enough for us to win the trophy.

I have to say I was over the moon because of the achievement. I considered it a real feather in the cap. Winning international matches with a national team is a great feeling but guiding a club side, especially one from Australia, to an international tournament victory was something else. To this day I regard the achievement as one of the greatest of my career.

Having collected the first trophy by an Australian club in a major international tournament, we returned to Sydney to be greeted at the airport by several hundred St George fans. We revelled in the euphoria, but underneath the veneer, I was a little more subdued.

The tournament had only served to enhance the pressure on the club to win the championship. The players had set the benchmark and now nothing less than the title would do for me, the players, the officials and the fans.

We started the season strongly, but we were hit by a sledgehammer when Johnny Warren, who, at 27, was really on top of his form at that stage, suffered his crippling knee injury. I remember the day vividly. It was in a match against Prague at Wentworth Park.

John admitted later that his knee just buckled beneath him. At first there were some who blamed Raul Blanco, an Argentine who settled in Australia and went on to become a top flight club coach in the National Soccer League and right-hand man at junior and national team level to the likes of Les Scheinflug, Eddie Thomson and Terry Venables.

Despite John's absence, something the critics said the club would not overcome, we finished runner-up to Hakoah in the League but, unlike in Europe where the champions are determined by the more conventional and time-honoured first-past-the-post, the title was decided via a finals playoff series. While the latter system ultimately benefited St George—we went on to beat Western Suburbs 3–2 in the grand final—I have never been in favour of it.

Soccer in this country has flirted on and off over the years between the first-past-the-post and finals playoffs formats, but has stuck rigidly to the traditional Australian sporting way with grand finals deciding the champions for the last 20 years or so of the old National League and now the A-League.

I have won titles both ways but nothing will change my mind in this matter. For me, the true worth of a team can only truly be measured through what it achieves throughout the season. Playing consistently over two full rounds, overcoming injuries, suspensions, weather conditions, etc is the real test of a club—not a one-off match which could be decided by a team having a bad day, a poor refereeing decision, a piece of bad luck or a fluke.

Having said that, I am not going to be silly enough now to suggest Hakoah was the true champion of 1971!

As incredible as it may sound, I left St George within 24 hours of the grand final win and joined the Italian-orientated Marconi, a very ambitious club in Sydney's fast growing south western suburbs and an organisation that would go on to achieve remarkable success in Australian club football notably in the National Soccer League.

The whole drama had a knock on effect and was a catalyst for the serious falling-out between Arok and myself. St George called on Frank to return to Australia to take over after I had walked out. Sadly, he was fed some wrong information and that soured our relationship.

Make no mistake, while I was at St George for just a season I had quickly grown to love the club. There was something special about the place. Having to leave was one of the toughest moments of my football career. But there was a principle involved.

Among it all, I had other things to occupy my mind, notably the national team. Johnny's injury was a bitter blow for St George and a crippling, but not an insurmountable one for the Socceroos.

With John now out of action, I needed to find a replacement as captain for the national team. There was never any doubt who that man would be—Peter Wilson. I had been watching Peter closely for some time now.

I saw an imposing figure, a man mountain, a man who never asked for respect but got it anyway. He was a player's man. Peter was such a dominant player in defence and a truly wonderful leader.

Peter's first game as Socceroos captain was in mid-June, when an English FA squad, minus many name players, toured Australia for games in Sydney and Melbourne. The English squad included players such as Mick Mills (Ipswich), Peter Hindley (Nottingham Forest) and Ken Wagstaffe (Hull). Wagstaffe later coached Victorian club, George Cross.

I was also hamstrung by player absences. Of course, Warren was out injured as was Jimmy Mackay. Manfred Schaefer was unavailable because of business commitments, while some players like Dennis Yaager had simply lost form.

Both games resulted in 1–0 losses. In Sydney, John Watkiss was fabulous, but we got very tired in the second half and the FA scored pretty early in that half. In Melbourne, Wilson made one mistake and we were punished badly.

However, the Melbourne game was a vast improvement and there were a host of players who performed exceptionally well, especially Max Tolson, Jack Reilly, George Keith and Ray Baartz.

Despite that mistake, Peter was superb in both games, marshalling his defence and leading by example. A new leader had been born.

It was Israel's turn to tour here later in the year during a difficult time for us given that the season had ended, the players had let themselves go a little and the weather was starting to really warm up.

But I would not allow them to have any excuses. While I was

still getting the basis of the team in my mind, there was a lot of work ahead though I have to admit that things were starting to fall into place fairly well.

Thankfully, Mackay was available again after returning from a back problem, but Schaefer and John Watkiss were unavailable. I called in goalkeeper Roger Romanowicz and the veteran Frank Micic, who hadn't played for the national team for four years.

Israel had most of its big guns available, including the inspirational midfielder and captain Mordechai Spiegler, goalkeeper Itzik Visoker, Zvi Rosen, Yehoshua Feigenbaum, Itzhak Shum and Yehuda Shaharabani.

For the first game in Brisbane on November 11, I gave Tolson, Jimmy Rooney, Alan Ainslie and George Harris their A international debuts and I recalled Billy Vojtek, despite the problems of the 1970 world tour.

Big Maxy, who was to go on to play a significant role during the World Cup qualifiers, scored on debut and the match ended in a 2–2 draw. Vojtek showed his class with a fantastic display.

Of the game, Harry Davis, the then Sports Editor of Brisbane's *Courier Mail* newspaper wrote, 'A crowd of 8000 saw the type of football which, if a replay were possible next week, would draw 25 000 people just by word-of-mouth acclaim. The Australians played all over Israel, the country with World Cup experience. The amazingly fit, young Australian side outpaced and outmanoeuvred the visitors in all departments. Australian soccer proved on Thursday night that we are in world class.'

We did not play as well in the second match in Sydney and were probably fortunate to get away with a 1–0 win thanks to a super long range strike from Ainslie. The Israelis missed some very good scoring chances, but I bet not too many people would remember that!

I gave Ernie Campbell and Brian Turner (both as substitutes) their A international debuts in the third match at Olympic Park in Melbourne on November 21 but this was a disastrous result for us. We were comprehensively beaten 3–1.

Of course, the end of a series would not be complete without some fun from the players, who were allowed to go out on the town and celebrate what was generally a job well done.

This time it was manager Ian Brusasco's turn to be on the receiving end. The players loaded the usually serious Brusasco's suitcase with condoms as a parting gift.

With the Socceroos in limbo for a little while, I concentrated on my job with Marconi. The club had won promotion into the NSW division one in 1970 and after struggling in 1971 it decided to go all out to ensure it would become one of the high fliers of the code in this country.

Marconi already had the basis of a very good squad with the likes of Ray Richards, Ernie Campbell, Bill Rorke, John Roche and Alfredo Moschen. But I shored it up further by signing Wilson and Tolson from South Coast United for a total cost of $8700. Incredibly, I resold Peter to South Coast (then called Safeway United) after one season for $10 000 and Max followed a year later for $4000. Now that is shrewd business!

It was to be a fabulous season with Marconi. Luckily, the club had a terrific board led by chairman of soccer, Carlo Zaccariotto, with whom I formed a great friendship, and members Ronny Cavagnino and Costanzo Nicomede. They were not typical of soccer administrators. They never interfered with what I wanted to do and stuck to the adage that administrators are best seen, not heard.

In my first season at the club, Marconi finished second in the 1972 championship but won the Australian club championship, which was the pinnacle. The tournament included the four leading teams from Victoria and NSW. Thanks to a Tolson goal we beat St George 1–0 in the final though the Saints got some revenge a week later, beating us 3–2 in the Federation Cup after goalkeeper Jim Fraser saved a Ray Richards penalty.

Another great result was a 0–0 draw with Czechoslovakian club side Slovan Bratislava in February 1972, continuing proof of the vast improvement in playing standards in Australian football.

During the season the Socceroos got back into the swing of things and the campaign was marked by some controversy, notably surrounding the first appearance in Australia of the Brazilian great, Pele.

But first we had to play Scotland's Dundee, a club which was not in the top echelon back home but which still managed to beat us 2–1. This was a game our goalkeeper Roger Romanowicz will never forget.

Playing in front of his home crowd in Adelaide, poor Roger was awe struck. He went to pieces. From a Dundee corner he managed to punch the ball into his own net and the game was only a few minutes old.

Then about 10 minutes later he came out to cover a cross but only fumbled it into the path of a Dundee player and before we knew it we were 2–0 down against a side that went on to win all seven matches on tour. While Adrian Alston scored for us midway through the first half, it wasn't enough, though we had Dundee under all sorts of pressure for the rest of the game.

Sadly, that was the end of Roger's Socceroos career. Unfortunately, there was no room for sentiment or forgiveness as far as I was concerned. There were far better goalkeepers like Jack Reilly, Jim Fraser, Jim Milisavljevic and Alan Maher ahead of him.

Then came two games against English club Wolverhampton Wanderers, one of the giants of the game over there at the time. Wolves boasted a huge array of talent at the time, including goalkeeper Phil Parkes (who played one match for England), Irishman Derek Dougan (capped 43 times for Northern Ireland), Derek

Parkin and Frank Munro (who ended up playing with South Melbourne), Jim McCalliog and Alan Sunderland. They were coached by Sammy Chung.

I remember Chung was quoted in one of the newspapers before the game saying his side was not here for a holiday and that they would be unrelenting against us and looking for a big result.

It made the 1–0 win at Olympic Park on June 11 even more satisfying. Ray Richards, George Harris and Manfred Schaefer were outstanding. Bogdan 'Bugsey' Nyskohous made a nice debut coming on as a substitute. Atti Abonyi scored the winner five minutes from fulltime after Jimmy Rooney typically refused to give up, chased down a ball, forced a mistake then delivered a great pass to Abonyi to score.

The return match two days later at the old Sydney Sports Ground, where more than 16 000 turned up to watch what was an exciting affair. We showed the first result was no fluke by drawing 2–2 after Ray Baartz had scored twice only for McAlle and Hugh Curran to equalise each time.

It wasn't long before Pele-mania struck soon after as his Brazilian club side Santos arrived in town for a hit-and-run visit.

The Brazilian magician caused a huge media fuss. You only had to pick up a newspaper or turn on the television or radio and he was being featured. But it should be remembered, Santos also included some wonderful players such as Ze Carlos, Leao, Nene, Jader Goncalves and Edu.

This was going to be a huge test for the Socceroos. But the June 17 game almost didn't take place. Santos had been told they would receive $US36 000 as their fee to play the game. It was to be paid by 10.30am on the day of the game, but they were only given part of the fee by 12.30pm.

Santos officials dug their toes in. They wanted all the money in American dollars by the time they left their hotel room to go to the ground. As it was a Sunday there were no banks open. A lot of strings had to be pulled by frantic ASF officials.

In the meantime the crowd of almost 32 000, unaware of the dramas, was restless. There was a lot of slow handclapping and jeers as the 3pm kick-off passed with no sign of the players. Eventually, the money was found, the game kicked off and those at the ground witnessed a magic day for Australian football.

I believe everyone who attended that day held long and endearing memories of the match. Probably the thing that sticks out most in my memory is the performance of Richards.

There had been a lot of conjecture before the game about who would be given the role of marking the great Pele. It was assumed Mackay was the frontrunner for he was a marvellous marker who had done the job of such noted players as Greece's Domazos and Spiegler of Israel.

Ray was determined he would be the man to be given the job and he continually pestered me to make a decision. This went on for weeks before Santos arrived. Whenever he saw me in the lead-up he would want to talk about the game and Pele. I knew from the start who I wanted, but I wasn't going to let on. I wanted to keep all the players on their toes. Everyone was breaking their neck just to play let alone marking Pele.

I knew from Ray's persistence that he was ready for the job. Came the day of the match and I named the starting XI at the team hotel in Coogee before we left for the ground. But none of the players knew what their specific roles would be.

It wasn't until team liaison officer, (the late) Kevin D'arcy, knocked on our dressing room door to tell us the referee was ready to go out on to the field that I pulled Ray aside and told him he had the job.

I remember my exact words to him, 'You have your wish. You will mark Pele but I warn you—if you kick him I'll take you off and if you don't mark him close enough I'll take you off as well.' I guess I didn't give him much room to move, but I knew he could do it. The bigger the game, the better he played.

Ray's reaction caught me a little unawares. While he was a hard, uncompromising man on the field, off it he was a mild mannered person. But it still surprised me when he went quiet for about 90 seconds before rushing to the toilet to be violently ill.

Ray was superb, absolutely stunning as we drew 2-2 with the Brazilians. Yes, Pele got away a few times during the game, but no-one in the world could have stopped him. Ray had done his job, so much so that Pele heaped praise on him after the match and described him as one of the best markers he had played against.

Ray was so proud of what he achieved that day that he eventually got a licence number plate for his car with the word Pele. I can tell you that car was a common sight in Fairfield for some time after that game.

Chapter 9
Playing on the Edge

With the World Cup qualifiers due in 1973, time was starting to run out and there was a sense of urgency and excitement as the team prepared for what was to be a beneficial, controversial and, at times, frightening tour of Asia.

I will carry some of the memories of that 1972 tour, which marked the international comeback of John Warren following his knee injury, to my grave for there were things that happened that would have forced travelling sporting teams to turn around and go home immediately. At one stage that almost happened.

It started conventionally enough. We had a fairly routine 4–1 win over Indonesia at the Senayan Stadium in Jakarta on October 7 in which Bobby Hogg and Branko Buljevic made their A-international debuts and Warren came on as a substitute for Jimmy Mackay. John didn't do anything out of the ordinary but he was back in the green and gold and he looked a happy man. He was entitled to be delighted for many back home had doubted he would play again, let alone turn out for the Socceroos.

In stifling conditions, we beat New Zealand 3–1 at the same stadium three days later with Dougie Utjesenovic making his first appearance for the Socceroos in an A-international.

We then flew to South Vietnam for a game against the Vietnamese under 23s. It was the height of the Vietnam War. Gough Whitlam, with whom I had become mates, had become prime minister of Australia and was there to see our troops pull out of the war.

We were based at the Miramar Hotel in Saigon (now Ho Chi Min City) and were surprised by the absence of security. We were told there was no need for it. Of course, we were all more than a little apprehensive about the situation but there was nothing we could do at the time.

The Vietnamese were trying all sorts of tricks to put us off our game, including pouring tons of sand on to the playing surface of the Cong Hoa Stadium and rolling it to make it very hard and uncomfortable for us.

We were expected to win easily, but I warned the players to be careful. The Vietnamese were quick and skilful, but our strength and speed should be too much for them to handle. I especially asked the players not to foul their opponents too often.

Well, the Vietnamese caused us a few problems. They were playing well and they made some of the guys look silly by taking them on with the ball then skipping past them. Bobby Hogg and Manfred Schaefer, a granite hard man with a powerful physique and intimidating presence, took exception and they were involved in a few rugged fouls that did not go down well with the home crowd.

After a tough struggle we got the better of them and won 2–0. But more was to come. The crowd wasn't happy. They rioted. Rocks, debris and other missiles hailed down on the field. The players were stunned and were momentarily stranded out in the middle of the stadium before being ushered under the grandstand and into what we thought was the safety of the dressing room.

However, as team representative, Tom Patrick, was rushing for

Top left: Mates forever. At age 17(right) with my orphanage friend Milan Galic in 1954 when playing with Proleter.

Top right: Proud day. Wearing my first Yugoslavian jersey in 1953.

Bottom: What a day. I'm fifth from the left before playing for Yugoslavia under 18s against Hungary in 1954.

Top: Helping out. Protecting my goalkeeper for Spartak against mighty Red Star in 1958.

Bottom right: The boss. Coaching Footscary JUST in 1969.

Bottom left: Great legs. Training for Spartak. The grass needed a good mow!

Oh, the strain. On the bench during my stint as coach of Victoria in 1968.

My long time assistant Les Scheinflug looks the part before we played Greece in Athens in 1970.

With Hungarian legend Ferenc Puskas in Greece in 1970.

Top: With Sandy Irvine (centre) and Jim Mackay (right) in Mexico in 1970.

Bottom: Greek tragedy. I respond at a dinner hosted by the Greek Football Federaton after Australia's win against the Greeks on the 1970 world tour.

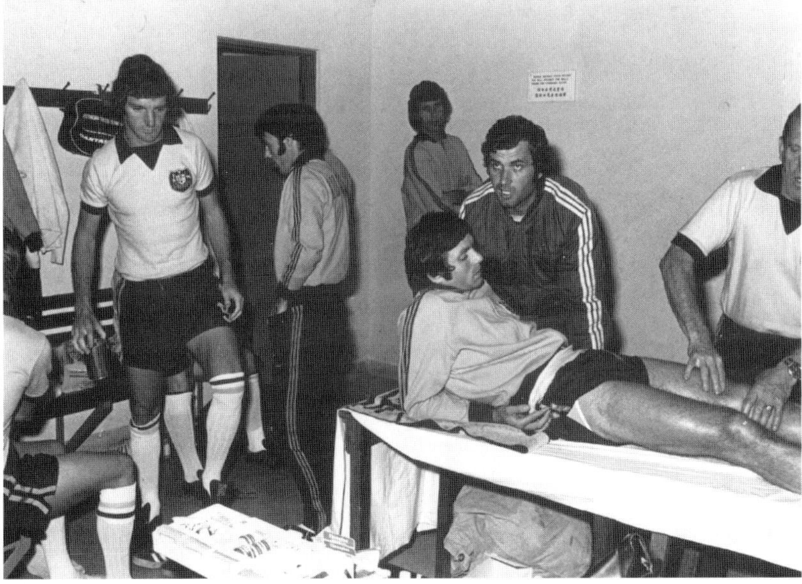

Top: What nerves? On the team bus on the way to the play-off against South Korea in 1973. We won 1–0 and qualified for the World Cup.

Bottom: Calm before the storm. Giving last minute instructions to Doug Utjesenovic, while Ray Baartz (left) and Jimmy Rooney (centre) are in deep thought before the historic 1–0 win against South Korea.

I became friends with Gough Whitlam in the 1970s, here pictured before we played against Uruguay at the SCG in 1974.

shelter, someone threw a plastic bag of kerosene, which was used by the myriad food vendors at the ground, at him, striking him in the face.

It was a terribly nasty situation and I'll never forget the sight of team doctor Brian Corrigan literally pouring buckets of water into Tom's eyes. By now there was incredible fear. It was in everyone's eyes, including the toughest of our tough players.

At this stage, a large number of fans found their way outside our dressing room. Again they hurled rocks and missiles, breaking numerous windows and causing us to duck for cover under anything we could find. Once it was thought it was safe, we made our way to the team bus only to be greeted by more raging fans and more missiles and rocks.

The team bus was pummelled. A rock smashed a window next to Peter Wilson. Luckily, an Australian flag, which had been placed across the window, saved Peter from very serious injuries. Glass splattered everywhere and had it not been for the flag, he could quite easily have been blinded or badly hurt.

All hell broke loose once we got back to the hotel. As far as the players were concerned, that was the end of the Vietnamese leg of the tour and they would not be playing the last game against the national team.

In a bid to change their mind, the players were made all sorts of promises about better security arrangements, including 2000 troops to be stationed in and around the stadium. But not even the Australian ambassador could sway them.

In the end, it took a remarkably emotional plea from team physiotherapist, Peter Van Ryn, a Dutchman who had adopted Australia as his home and had been with the Socceroos since 1970, to change the minds of the players.

Peter, a real character who had become an integral member of the close-knit squad and would do anything and everything for them, had been badly shaken by the after-match events and no-one would have blamed him if he wanted to go home. But Peter spoke from the heart when he stood up in front of the players. He spoke about the Aussie spirit, about how we don't give up and how we fight in adversity.

The players voted to continue with the leg of the tour and went on to beat South Vietnam 1–0, thanks to a Branko Buljevic goal. This time there wasn't even a hint of trouble.

Next stop was South Korea where we were to play two games against the national team in Seoul. It has to be said that it was a relief to move on. Certainly the players showed it and, with their spirits lifted, it didn't take them long to get involved in the practical jokes. This time tour leader, (the late) Karol Rodny, was on the receiving end.

Karol was a very passionate man about his football and dedicated much of his life to the sport. He was president of the NSW Soccer Federation and had a long association with Prague, one of the leading clubs in NSW.

It was Karol's task to look after the passports of the touring squad. On arrival at the airport in South Korea, we all assembled at the baggage carousel to collect our luggage. Karol had all the passports and other valuables in a small bag which he tucked safely between his legs while helping to collect all the gear.

One by one and in short intervals, the players would come behind him and tap him on the shoulder. This would cause him to open his legs and release the valuables bag. As soon as he did that, the player would pick up the bag and put it on the carousel with Karol chasing frantically after it. This happened a few times and I can tell you he was one frustrated man in the end.

Peter Wilson, who had cemented his spot by this time, was the centre of a couple of incidents. At the time long hair was frowned on in South Korea and this was a problem for Peter, who was renowned for his flowing, long blond locks. It was decided he would wear a wig when we arrived at the airport to prevent any dramas with local officials.

He got through okay but caused a commotion in the first match when the fans saw his long hair. There was a real hum around the ground when they spotted him and Peter made sure they did...he continually put his hands through his hair and shock it whenever he could.

A tall, solidly built man, Peter was also quite good looking and, understandably, attracted a lot of female attention. An American band was staying at the same hotel as us and had a very attractive female lead singer. She was smitten by Peter and had attended the game.

After the game, she asked to be put through to Peter's room, but the call was put to Atti Abonyi's room instead. I was having a chat with Atti at the time. He answered the phone and realised who it was straight away. 'I think it is the American singer,' he said to me. 'She wants to speak to Willy. What will I do?'

I thought I'd have some fun at Peter's expense. I told Atti I would hide in the wardrobe and that he should get Peter to come to the phone. Peter came in and took the phone and, apparently, she asked Peter to go out with her, but he answered, 'Darling, it is like this. I have a c... of a coach who will send me on the first flight home if I do anything wrong.' At that point I came out of the wardrobe. Peter looked surprised and said, 'Just as well I didn't say anything wrong.' Anyway, we all had a great laugh.

The first game finished in a 1–1 draw (Max Tolson scored) before we beat them 2–0 in the return match with Ray Baartz and Jim Armstrong scoring. Baartz was lucky to play in that game.

He had dislocated his shoulder in the first match and the team doctor had, without telling him, ruled him out. I needed Ray to play in the second match. I took him for a walk two days before the game and told him he was out of the match.

'Who says?' he asked. 'The team doctor.' I replied. 'Well fuck the doctor,' he said before tearing off the mountain of strapping on his shoulder. Ray played and scored. That tells you a lot about the toughness and dedication of the man.

It was in Seoul where tour leader Rodny started talking to a Scottish sailor in the hotel restaurant. We watched as the sailor spun him a story of how he had been robbed of all his money and jewellery, except for the one ring on his finger. The sailor continually flashed the ring in front of Karol, who was always on the lookout for a bargain. The sailor had told him he did not know what to do and all he wanted was to go back home.

Being a kind man, Karol, who by this time was fascinated by the ring, asked the sailor if he wanted to sell the ring to make some money so he could get home and how much he would want for it. The sailor relented. Karol bought it for $250, which was big money in those days. Karol could not stop talking about his bargain and how good the ring was. He continually flashed it around in the presence of everyone. During a stop over in Hong Kong, Karol visited a jeweller shop to have the ring valued, only to be shattered when told it was made of high-class glass and worth nothing.

When he arrived back at the hotel he contacted me and said, 'Sack every fucking Scotsman in the squad!' The boys had a bit of fun with that one.

We had one more match, a stop-over game in Manila, where we beat the Philippines 6–0. The tour had been a fantastic experience. We encountered a lot of obstacles and dramas, but we came through it a better squad.

We were prepared for everything, and we had to be for we were to play three more lead-up games—a series against the visiting Bulgaria in February 1973—before the World Cup qualifiers. The

Bulgarians had sent their second string side and only two players, Georgi Vassiliev and Atanas Mikhailov, went on the play at the 1974 World Cup finals. But they were still a very classy bunch.

After a good first up 2–2 draw in Sydney in what was a rugged affair in which referee Tony Boskovic was forced to step in a number of times, we lost the next two matches 3–1 in Adelaide and 2–0 in Melbourne. It was disappointing, but I wasn't too concerned. This was great preparation for what really counted, the World Cup qualifiers.

The Melbourne match marked the debut of goalkeeper, Jimmy Fraser, who I still regarded as one of our greatest goalkeepers. Jimmy was a wonderful character, and still is, and a much loved member of the squad. Unfortunately, his international career was hamstrung by business commitments.

Now, came the moment of truth—the World Cup qualifiers.

In my mind, I had done everything possible to get the team to where I wanted. Everything had been planned almost to the minute. Incredibly, Australian soccer was working together. A unified nation. Even the Australian Soccer Federation had bent over backwards to ensure the best possible preparation.

The qualification process started at the Newmarket ground in Auckland on March 4 1973 with a game against traditional rivals New Zealand. The Kiwis had not had anywhere near the preparation we had and were not expected to put up much of a fight. However, as Australian teams in every sport have discovered to their dismay and disappointment over the years, the Kiwis perform like supermen and women whenever they play against Australia.

This was like a World Cup final for New Zealand and they had us under pressure for most of the game, especially when Brian Turner scored a shock goal in the 57th minute. While Dougie Utjesenovic was having a whale of a game, others struggled. I had to do something in the second half so I replaced Tolson with

Ernie Campbell and brought on Abonyi for Warren.

Campbell saved us some huge embarrassment by scoring five minutes from fulltime. It came after a goalmouth scramble and it wasn't the prettiest goal by any stretch of the imagination. But it was pure gold for us. The goal was our signature tune. Again, it highlighted our never-say-die attitude, something that was to really come to the fore as the qualifying process gathered momentum.

The next game against Iraq at the Sydney Sports Ground gave us a comfortable 3–1 win. I have to admit, I received a huge amount of help, notably from my great mate, Lou Brocic, who provided me with an 11-page dossier on the Iraqi players. I knew everything about our opponents—their temperament, weaknesses and best shooting foot.

Interestingly, Lou had underlined, in thick red ink, one sentence in his dossier. The Iraqis never wore screw in studs, meaning they rarely played in wet conditions.

Well, their players could barely hold their feet on the slippery Sports Ground surface. Adrian Alston with two goals and Ray Richards scored in a victory that was a tremendous boost, a great result brought about by a combination of factors. The coaching staff, psychologists and groundsmen had all done their jobs!

Two days later we played Indonesia in Sydney and won 2–1. It was far from an impressive performance, but goals from Campbell and Alston were enough to give us the valuable points and set us up for the return match against the Kiwis in Sydney on March 16.

The game against New Zealand was there for the taking, especially when we raced to a 3–1 lead after just 26 minutes. Alan Vest, who coached Perth Glory in the inaugural A-League and the man who was to be earmarked as Socceroos coach in 1975, scored the opening goal by chipping goalkeeper Ron Corry before Utjesenovic, Baartz and Buljevic scored to give us what should have been a comfortable margin.

We played some superb football but, as you would expect, the Kiwis refused to lie down and die. They scored twice in the last 10 minutes through Ron Tindall and an own goal from Bobby Hogg to force a 3–3 draw in a result that shocked us back to reality. This was World Cup football and no game should be taken for granted.

It was now down to the nitty gritty, a return game against Iraq in Melbourne. The Iraqis were the danger side for us. It was imperative we did not lose this game. And we didn't. The 0–0 draw wasn't pretty but it was good enough for us. The Iraqis complained about our style of football and likened it to rugby. But this was not a one-sided thing. They gave as much as they got and, besides, we were playing for high stakes.

In our last match, we thumped poor Indonesia 6–0 in Sydney with Mackay and Abonyi each grabbing a brace of goals. With three wins and three draws Australia was through to the next stage, just a point ahead of Iraq. The draw in Melbourne had indeed done the job.

The World Cup was getting closer, but there was still a lot of work to be done. While I was happy with the first qualification series the truth is we played on the edge at times. The game against New Zealand was a real wake-up call. We were almost eliminated at the first hurdle. We were to discover it was just the start of the tightrope walk for us.

Our next opponents were Iran, which was to prove a real thorn in the side of Australian soccer not just in this series but 24 years down the track. I'm sure no-one will ever forget what they did to Australia in the return leg World Cup qualifier at the Melbourne Cricket Ground in 1997.

Strangely, however, they did not pose too many problems for us in the first leg at the Sydney Sports Ground on August 18, where more than 30 000 fans turned up to watch us win 3–0.

We were ready for the Iranians, that's for sure. They had played two warm-up matches in New Zealand on the way to Sydney, but it was a disaster for them as they lost their key midfielder and star player, Ali Parvin. The New Zealand games against provincial sides also gave me the chance to dispatch several spies to watch them train and play.

By the time they hit town we knew everything about them. All the information was collated and handed to the players. I had the photos of every Iranian player plastered on the walls of the hotel at Wahroonga. I put aside the photos of the 11 Iranians I thought would start the game and told my players who were assigned to mark them to study their faces. We listed their strengths and weaknesses, best kicking foot, whether they were good in the air or not. In the end I think we knew more about them they knew about themselves!

To be honest, we did not play all that well in the first leg. Our midfield was almost non-existent. Richards, Mackay and Warren were way below their best form, but thankfully Utjesenovic and Curran were brilliant in overlapping down the wings.

Abonyi was also tremendous and he scored a fantastic goal just seconds into the second half which was a just reward for his efforts. Alston and Wilson also scored to give us what we thought was a very comfortable advantage going into the second leg in Tehran. We should have won by far more, to be honest, but three would be enough…or so we thought!

Both teams travelled to Tehran on the same flight but I told the players they were not to talk to their opponents at all. I could see the Iranians were down in the dumps and they were in no mood for talking anyway. The loss hurt them badly and I suspect they knew what they were in for once they landed back at home.

Sure enough, there were thousands of fans at the airport to protest against their team's poor showing. Both teams were ushered out of the airport via a back entrance and on to the same bus, which detoured around the fans and got us safely to the hotel.

The protests over and done with, the fans soon forgot about their team's poor performance and started to try and put the pressure back on us. Everywhere we went, the fans would put up four fingers...the number of goals they said their side would score to knock us off. They were supremely confident.

Not long after arriving in Tehran I had to attend a press conference at the Hotel Intercontinental and the local media zeroed in on the fact we had brought our own food. Sound familiar? Former Soccer Australia chairman, David Hill, got himself into hot water in 1997 when it became known the Socceroos were taking their own drink supplies to Iran for the first leg World Cup qualifier and would then bring in their own food from Dubai, where they would be based until 24 hours before the match. It made national headlines and Hill was rebuked by a procession of Iranian leaders.

Well, I can tell you the reaction was just as bitter and controversial in 1973! I did not want to leave anything to chance. We had put ourselves into a near unbeatable position and I did not want to risk sabotage. We took our own meat, vegetables, milk and water.

I was bombarded with question after question on the food issue and I tried to deflect it by saying our team was very inexperienced and always found it difficult to adjust to different climates, time zones and food. But they kept on and on and eventually I had enough.

Regretfully, I snapped back, 'Look gentleman, I represent a superior race. In Australia, we eat Australian steak; we don't import US steak like you do.' The reaction was instant. The next day the newspaper headline screamed, 'The man that wasn't born in Australia represents a superior race.' The psychological battle was on in earnest.

As if there wasn't enough on my plate by now, another drama

unfolded a day before the game. Former *Daily Mirror* and *Daily Telegraph* journalist Tom Anderson, who was covering the game, gave me some information that sent me into a rage.

By this time we had learned that the winner between us and Iran would have to play South Korea in a home and away series to determine which country would go to the World Cup finals. Unbeknown to me ASF representative, Vic Tuting, who was meeting with two FIFA vice-presidents and a South Korean official on the fifth floor of our hotel, had agreed that if the games against the South Koreans were deadlocked after the two matches then the third would be held a week later in Hong Kong.

This did not suit me at all. Australian teams had a huge advantage over their Asian opponents through their physical prowess and far better fitness. It would be to our advantage to have the third game, if required, played as soon as possible, preferably 72 hours later. Bloody officials! There was no consultation with me at all. They just went ahead and did what they pleased without looking at all sides.

Again, I snapped. I charged up to the fifth floor and hammered on the door where the meeting was being held. Vic told me to get out of the room. The FIFA officials were angry too and threatened to have me suspended because I had no right to be in the room and the South Korean guy was angrily pointing his finger at me.

I stood my ground and told the officials that, as the coach of the Australian team, I had the full say on what happens with the team and that Vic was in no condition to deal with them and make decisions. I told them I would not leave until the matter was resolved. It was a huge game of bluff, but I was always a good poker player!

I got my way and it was to prove one of the pivotal administrative fights and victories of my coaching career. The third game would be 72 hours later. Sadly, the victory came at a cost. Vic and

I had harsh words later. We never spoke to each other again. After arriving back in Sydney after the second leg he even insisted that I be sacked on the spot.

Vic, however, was the least of my problems in Tehran for the match itself at the incredible Aryamehr Stadium and was a remarkable, nerve-jangling 90 minutes of roller-coaster emotions. It was both the worst and best moment of my career. Even now no 1974 Socceroos re-union is complete without memories of that game being brought up.

I started with the same XI I used in Sydney while the Iranians, who must have felt 10 feet tall with the huge support of more than 100 000 fanatical fans behind them, made four changes. The support soon did the trick for we were on the back foot from the 15th minute when Parvis Ghelichkhani scored from the penalty spot after the Russian referee, who was to be a real thorn in our side, decided that Richards had handled the ball.

By this stage the players were stunned. It was very hot and they were complaining they could not breathe. The fanatical support, the referee and the conditions were making it almost impossible for us and I admit I wondered to myself several times whether we would get out of trouble.

The nerves became almost unbearable and the support even wilder when Iran went ahead 2–0 after 31 minutes when the irrepressible Ghelichkhani unleashed a thunderbolt 25-metre drive that gave our goalkeeper, Jimmy Fraser, absolutely no chance. By this time Jim had let in two goals, through no fault of his own, but was still our saviour. He had a phenomenal game and made save after save.

It did not help my demeanour that as each goal went in an Iranian sideline commentator would come up to me and ask sarcastically, 'What now Mr Rasic?' I looked him in the eyes and with all the bravado I could muster I fired back, 'Australia to qualify!'

The situation now called for drastic measures. It was close to half-time and I pulled Max Tolson aside and told him he was to verbally and physically attack Adrian Alston at half-time. I wasn't happy with Adrian because he wasn't putting in, but I also wanted to shock all the players into action.

I spoke first at half-time and told the players we were still leading 1–0 (we had won the first leg 3–0 so it was still 3–2 our way on aggregate). Then it was Maxy's turn. Well, you have never seen anything like it.

He got stuck into Adrian, telling him he was nothing but a bloody 'Pommy c…' and he didn't deserve to play in an Australian jersey as he grabbed at his shirt, almost tearing it off him. 'That's not the way you play for my country!' Tolson said. Adrian, the joker of the squad, was stunned and the players were incredulous.

Max then turned to the players and said, 'Follow me, I'll show you how it is done.' I took over again and told them what we would do straight from the kick off. 'Send the ball right to Johnny (Warren). He will put in a high cross into the six-yard box. Let their keeper collect the ball, but, at the same time I want Max to challenge him and whoever else is in his way.'

Well, it was like World War 3 had erupted. Right on cue, Max arrived at the same time the keeper collected the high cross. The goalkeeper, two defenders and Max ended up in the back of the net, a tangled mess of legs and arms. There were moans and groans coming from the Iranians, who did not know what had hit them.

I ran on to the field and, fearful that the referee would send Max off, raced straight for him. Max, a tough nut if ever there was one, was about to get up, but I put my foot on his arm and rubbed my boot studs as hard as I could. He let out an almighty scream and asked, 'What in the fuck are you doing?' I told him, 'Stay down, stay down or the referee will send you off.' Amazingly, the ploy worked. The referee did not even issue him a caution!

Max's job was far from finished, however. I had told him during the break that if we hadn't scored after 15 minutes of the second half he was to drop back and help the defence. I wanted *catenaccio*, an almost impregnable defensive style adopted by the Italians who were the masters at protecting very close leads this way.

After 15 minutes he dropped back in to the defence and that wasn't all. At one stage I saw him with his hands around the throat of Gholamhossen Mazloumi. He was yelling and screaming, 'I'm going to fucking kill you!' Needless to say, Mazloumi went missing for the rest of the match. He switched from the left to the right flank but never in the middle where Maxy was just waiting for him.

In the last 30 minutes our defence was superb, rock solid. Not even an army would have broken through them. Fraser, Wilson, Utjesenovic, Watkiss, Curran, Richards stood 10 feet tall.

With 20 minutes to go, I told Rooney he was going on to replace Warren. But first I asked him what John was doing wrong. Jim replied, 'He is holding onto the ball too long.' I grabbed Jimmy by the shirt and told him, 'He is not holding it enough! Go out there, hold the ball, beat one man, beat two men and if there is no other defender in front of you kick the ball over the touch line.' I wanted Jimmy to hold the ball on the counter but not cross if we did not have anyone in the centre.

Jimmy went on and the first time he got the ball he beat one defender, then another then kicked the ball over the line satisfied he had done what I had asked. I stood up and clapped him mockingly. He had not done what I asked and I abused him. He was dumbfounded.

When I showed him a replay of the incident later, I asked him why he had kicked the ball over the line. 'Because you told me too,' he replied. I pointed out there was a third defender 25 metres away. He had to draw him as well then kick the ball over the line to waste time. Players need to think for every second of the match. Jimmy understood where I was coming from.

The Iranian result was out of this world. Yet again Australia had managed to dodge another bullet in the race for qualification. It seemed someone was looking after us.

Now only South Korea stood between us and destiny. Four years of hard work, passion and dedication would be decided by one hundred and eighty minutes of football.

Chapter 10

The Socceroos Make it at Last

DESPITE having been on the brink of extinction twice during the qualifiers, once against New Zealand then against Iran, expectations for the Socceroos were now very high. This was fuelled by huge local media interest.

You couldn't pick up a newspaper or listen to or watch a news bulletin without some mention of Australia's pending final qualification hurdle against South Korea. In the media's eyes, we had already qualified for the World Cup finals in Germany. South Korea would pose no problems, so they said. Fortunately, being a club coach as well, I was immune to all the talk, conjecture and analysis.

I completed my domestic duties by guiding Marconi to the NSW grand final success, a 2–1 win over Hakoah. It was a fine achievement and gave me huge satisfaction.

That helped me keep my senses. I needed to get away a little from the Socceroos. I needed something else to occupy my mind so that I could recharge the batteries for what was going to be the biggest moment in the history of Australian soccer.

While the media were playing down the Koreans' chances I knew better. While they finished second behind Israel in the preliminary Asian qualifiers, they went on to beat the other group winners Hong Kong in one semi-final while Israel beat Japan 1–0 in the other.

South Korea scored a goal in extra time in Seoul to knock off the highly fancied Israel to set up the final hurdle against Australia. The South Koreans had been well prepared. Expectations were also high for them after they beat Israel and their nation refused to believe they could lose against us.

For my part I was relatively confident about our prospects, though we had some problems in our final preparations due to the timing of the matches. We were out of season and had to prepare in the stifling heat and humidity.

We based ourselves for three weeks in our camp at Wahroonga. It was very hot and conditions were tough for the players, but they needed to be. We had to be physically and mentally tough. Unfortunately, we were restricted in the number of warm-up matches we could play. Club sides were not training so we were left to play the NSW under 23s once a week, sometimes twice a week.

I had them playing exactly the way I knew South Korea would play and they were a huge help. The side included the likes of the late and much loved Scotsman, Joe Watson, who played for Hakoah, later to be known as Eastern Suburbs Hakoah then Sydney City, and eventually for the Socceroos, plus Peter Stone and Terry Butler.

The players worked their butts off morning and afternoon and after one session I heard Mackay saying to good mate Rooney, 'It would be fucking nice to have a cold beer.' Even though I had banned alcohol I decided to put two bottles of beer in the fridge in the room they shared while they were out.

Now both Jimmys absolutely loved their beer; they would have been tempted to drink them immediately and they would not have touched the sides of their throats. But their conscience got the better of them. As soon as they found the beer they came down and saw me. They told me someone had put beer in their fridge.

I laughed. I told them I had given them the beer as a reward for training so hard and that they should go back to the room and I would send them another six bottles! How is that for honesty!

We were ready after the three weeks. South Korea had not managed to beat Australia in five games stretching back to 1967. Yes, they were skilful and quick players but, typically, they always had problems coping with our power and strength.

Again, I knew as much about the Koreans as they did about themselves. They had some quality players, including winger Cha Bum Keun, who held legendary status in his homeland, and a six-foot-two striker by the name of Kim Jae Han.

As the first game at the Sydney Sports Ground on October 28 approached, I was constantly trying to hose down the media and public expectations. It was a tough battle. Football is as much a psychological off-field battle as it is an on-field war. I needed the players to have their feet on the ground and their heads out of the clouds.

There was also another serious issue that needed to be dealt with just days before the match, one involving player payments. It was so serious that the game was almost called off though neither the media nor public suspected anything was wrong.

Having been ripped off so many times in the past by promises of this and that yet getting nothing or a pittance, the players were determined this time that they would not be played for fools by Arthur George and the ASF. I was told what was going on, but while I considered it very poor timing because it would affect the players' mental preparation, I told them they had to do what they had to do.

A few days before the match, a delegation of the most senior players in the squad, Peter Wilson, Ray Baartz, Ray Richards, John Watkiss, Manfred Schaefer and John Warren demanded to see

Arthur George. The players were extra smart in their timing because they knew the ASF would be powerless to do anything to them because of the closeness of the kick off date. Talk about bargaining power!

To this day the players still talk with fondness at how they got Arthur over a barrel. The ASF boss arrived on the Thursday with general secretary, Brian Le Fevre driving Arthur's Rolls Royce into the car park at Wahroonga.

The players got the same old spiel from Arthur. He gave them his word then said, 'Don't worry, we'll look after you.' Obviously he thought he could get away with it again. But the players were having none of it. They listened to him then asked to talk to the rest of the squad before returning two hours later to tell him of their decision. By this time Arthur was steaming because he had been made to wait two hours.

His mood grew considerably darker when the delegation told him the rest of the squad had rejected his offer. He stormed out yelling threats about sacking the players and bringing new ones in for the match. But somewhere between leaving us and reaching his car he had a change of heart. He got Le Fevre to drive around the block then returned and asked for another meeting.

This time he offered a percentage of the television rights and other revenue. The players were still sceptical, but they accepted the offer, happy in the knowledge they had made their point and scared the shit out of Arthur, who wasn't easy to fluster. To this day I believe Arthur thought I was the ring leader of all of this.

As for the game, even I have to admit we were extremely lucky to escape with a 0–0 draw. We were shocking and outplayed in every department. With Cha Bum Keun in devastating form, the Koreans served it up to us and probably should have scored two goals. And they would have scored had it not been for goalkeeper Fraser, who again stood tall.

Jimmy was in doubt for the match and needed to wear a huge bandage around his stomach to play. Jim wasn't that tall for a goal-keeper. In fact, he was rather on the short side, but what he lacked in height he made up for in faultless technique and courage. He is now goalkeeper coach at A-League club Sydney FC and one of the most respected and sought after keeper coaches in the country.

Having escaped from that situation, I was nonetheless confident about our prospects in the return leg in Seoul 13 days later on November 10. But first we had to overcome some more psycho-logical ploys from our opponents. In past trips to Seoul we were always ushered through customs without having to wait. It was a different story this time. We were made to wait almost three hours to be cleared through customs.

I didn't blame the Koreans. When you get this far you'll use any trick in the book to be successful. The trick is to know how to handle certain situations. As we waited for clearance, I instructed the players to start singing songs, any songs. Alston and Richards fancied themselves as singers and led the boys in a good, old sing-along that had the Korean officials looking on in utter bemuse-ment. They must have thought we were stark, raving mad.

Another big obstacle was the Korean weather. We were coming from a hot and humid Australian climate and Seoul was in the middle of a harsh winter. It was extraordinarily cold with rain, snow and hail.

And still the Koreans played the mind games. Under FIFA rules, visiting teams are allowed one training session at the match venue. When we turned up for our session the groundsman was just locking the entry gates. He refused to let us in, repeating in broken English, 'No, no. Finished.' He deemed the surface too wet, no doubt under instruction from someone up higher.

It's amazing, however, what money does. The equivalent of $50 was thrust into the palm of the groundsman. 'Ten minutes only,' he said. One hour later we were back on the bus and heading back to the hotel. Money does speak all languages.

More than 27 000 fans packed the stadium for the match. I made a number of changes bringing in Schaefer, who missed Sydney through injury, for Watkiss; and Rooney and Buljevic for Warren and Alston.

Incredibly, in the lead-up the South Korean coach had conducted a campaign through the local media instructing fans not to applaud if the Koreans scored a goal. It was a strange move and one I still don't understand to this day.

Well South Korea, as expected, threw everything at us. It was like a tidal wave. We had to somehow try and hold our nerve, but the home side was relentless. The first goal came after 15 minutes when Doug Utjesenovic's back-pass bounced off Fraser and at the feet of Kim Jae Han, who smashed the ball into the net. There was absolute silence in the ground. You could have heard a pin drop!

After 30 minutes it was 2–0. We failed to clear a cross in the penalty area and Ko Jae Wook unleashed a powerful shot that sailed in to the net off one of our defenders. Surely the crowd would erupt this time. No. Again there was silence.

At this stage team manager, John Barclay, who was sitting on the bench, turned to me and whispered, 'We are gone.' I couldn't believe my ears. Australians prided themselves on never giving up, on fighting to the end and here was a part of our Socceroos family telling me we couldn't win. I saw red.

John was a great mate, a gentleman, quiet and unassuming and he wasn't ready for my reaction. I grabbed him by both his arms and threw him off the bench! A minute later Buljevic gave us a lifeline by scoring with an unstoppable header from a pass from Col Curran, who had beaten two opponents. We were back in the game and John wanted to come back on the bench, but I was in no mood for forgiveness.

I wouldn't allow John back on the bench and when we walked to the dressing rooms at half-time I told him he would not be allowed in. I told the players what John had said during the first half and they deeply resented it as well. They were upset that he did not believe in them. To be honest, I was uncomfortable with what I did to John, but again psychology was playing a huge part. The boys needed a spur. They needed to be lifted and John was the sacrificial lamb.

My last words to the players before they went out for the second half was that I didn't care what the result was. '2–2, 3–2, 4–2, 5–2 for us. I don't care. We will not lose this game.'

Jimmy Rooney started the second half like a pocket dynamo. He was everywhere. The Koreans couldn't contain him. Just three minutes into the second half, Baartz unleashed one of his specials, a thunderbolt from about 15 metres which deflected off three Korean players before smashing in to the back of the net. Nothing was going to stop that ball from going in.

At 2–2 we were all over them. Wilson (twice), Alston and Buljevic hit the post in a game we could have won four or five to two. It was a remarkable comeback by remarkable players. The after-match celebrations were phenomenal. There wasn't a player or official who did not think we were bound for Germany.

Now my altercation with Tuting and the FIFA officials in Tehran took on huge significance. The third match would be played in Hong Kong 72 hours later. I told the players we were virtually on the way home and the Koreans were heading away from home. There was no way they were going to beat us in the third game.

The Koreans would be shattered, physically and mentally. They had the match in their keeping when they led 2–0. They were going to the World Cup. Now they had to play another match against a side brimming with confidence.

We left for Hong Kong that night and arrived at Le Gardens Hotel to be greeted by a huge throng of media. I could not help myself and continually told the press, 'We are unstoppable.' I was so confident.

The players, understandably, were knackered. They went straight to their rooms and rested before dinner. During dinner Mackay came to me and said that Rooney was ill and vomiting. I informed team doctor, Dr Scheps and his response was, 'Let me finish soup (then he would attend to Rooney).' Surprise, surprise, I blew up. 'Forget the bloody soup. Get the hell out of here and see how Jimmy Rooney is!' I shouted. He went off like a shot.

Training can usually give a coach a huge insight in to how their team, or your opponents, are shaping. It was music to my ears when my spies returned from South Korean training the next day and informed me six of their players had not trained because of knocks from the first match. On the other hand, my team was running around as if the second match had been a training run! I made no changes to my line-up but the Koreans were forced into three for the tiebreaker in front of 28 000 fans at Hong Kong Stadium on November 13, 1973—a day that will long be remembered in Australian sporting folklore.

As I walked through the tunnel for the match, our team liaison officer, Mr Yung, grabbed my hand, opened it, placed a chain with the number 13 on it and wished me luck. I put it in my tracksuit pocket and zipped it up. I found it three days later. I have never been one for jewellery and never wear much, but I have worn the chain ever since.

We dominated the game, but it wasn't until the 75th minute that pandemonium broke out. We received a free-kick just inside Korea's half and Richards swung the ball in the middle towards the penalty area. Rooney met the ball then chipped it back to his best mate, Mackay.

The rest seemed to be in slow motion. Mackay met the ball with a fierce volley from 30 metres out that sailed into the top left hand corner of the net, leaving their goalkeeper clutching at thin air. Time stood still for a few seconds both on the field and on our bench.

Then the place went crazy. It was the first time we had taken the lead in the series but unlike our opponents, we were not going to surrender. After a nervous final 15 minutes the fulltime whistle went. Again the bench was strangely subdued, wondering what to do next. That lasted all of 15 seconds before everyone raced on to the field to hug and embrace the players. I can remember being chaired off the field on the shoulders of Richards, Fraser, Wilson and others. I was 10 feet off the ground, but felt I could touch the stars.

The scenes in the dressing room later will remain with me forever. They were truly remarkable. Grown men were crying. There was laughter, songs, yahooing. The champagne flowed. Backslappers came from everywhere.

When we got back to Sydney, there were incredible scenes. We were mobbed by thousands of fans and what seemed as many media. My most vivid memory is Mackay being swamped by media photographers. He was plastered all over the television news and photographs of him holding his right boot and with his son, Malcolm, on his shoulders, were all over the newspapers the next day.

Australian soccer was now on the world sporting map. Surely, it would now find its niche on the local sporting scene alongside rugby league, Australian rules and cricket. It didn't, but that is another story.

After the dramas, controversy and euphoria of the World Cup qualifying campaign, life got back to some normality for me. Before leaving for the South Korean games and after winning the grand final with Marconi, I had agreed to terms with Greek-oriented club

Pan Hellenic, which later changed its name to Sydney Olympic.

Pan Hellenic was an ambitious club and president, Michael Isakidis, turned up at one of our training camps in Wahroonga one day in his Rolls Royce. His wife had followed him in a brand new Volvo. 'This is yours,' he said to me as he handed me the keys to the Volvo! We discussed the money side as well and an offer of $15 000 plus the car was mentioned.

But I decided to see how far I could go. '$15 000? Is that the down payment? How about another $10 000 on top of that?' Terms were agreed.

Michael and I took a trip to Greece and we spent time watching the big guns like Olympiakos, Panathinaikos and AEK train and we met with a number of Yugoslavian coaches.

Things turned a little sour when we got back to Sydney. Michael resigned six months later, though I stayed on for another two years. Pan Hellenic was super ambitious but officialdom held it back. It was why they never got success until many years later in the NSL.

Pan Hellenic aside, there was a lot to keep me occupied with the Socceroos. The media, especially from overseas, were very demanding, almost to the point of obsession. It was not uncommon to receive telephone calls from Germany, England and all parts of Europe, at all sorts of hours.

It was especially interesting talking to the English media, given the England side had failed to reach the finals. Much was made of the fact that a super football nation like England, who had won the World Cup just eight years earlier, was not in the finals this time and a country known more for the sun, beach, kangaroos, koalas and cricket was. It hurt the English pride even more with Scotland being in the finals as well.

How could this be? The critics pointed to FIFA's supposed unfair system of determining the 16 finalists. Why should Asia have a team in the World Cup at the expense of a European country? The predictable howls of protest were deafening. But I just laughed. Of course, you don't hear too many protests like that these days with the African and Asian nations emerging so rapidly and becoming a force.

To their credit, the German media were far more understanding (I think it thrived on the fact that long time rivals England would not be at the finals and we would). German television, radio and newspapers wouldn't leave me alone. They were desperate for any information about Australia, the country, and our football.

The next big event for the Socceroos wasn't a tour or match, but the draw for the World Cup finals in Frankfurt in January, 1974. Talk about glitz and glamour, pomp and ceremony!

I've seen some great events in my time but, at the time, this was simply amazing. It was breathtaking. I was like a kid in a lolly shop. Of course, the world media was very demanding and almost suffocating. But I didn't care about them for everywhere you looked there was a famous face, a former great player or coach, television and movie stars, officials. And here I was, mixing with them. I was in heaven.

Along with Brian Le Fevre, general secretary of the ASF, and Tom Patrick, the Qantas representative who was in charge of all our travel arrangements, we watched as the Socceroos were grouped with hosts West Germany, East Germany and Chile. Some called it a disaster. A group of death. I didn't agree. I was delighted to be honest.

I considered it a privilege and an honour to be in the same group as hosts West Germany. I was thinking of how much positive publicity Australian soccer would get. We would be matched against the two German sides and the eyes of the world would be focused on us. How good was that for a nation playing in its first World Cup finals?

While everyone was talking about West Germany, little was said about the East Germans. They were regarded as robots of the football world, clinical, hard-edged, supremely disciplined and very confident. They had not been beaten in 12 internationals stretching over two years.

Chile is a nation steeped in World Cup tradition and produced a fantastic effort to finish third at the 1962 finals after beating Yugoslavia 1–0 in the play-off for third and fourth.

The Australian delegation was continually on the go in Germany. We flew to Hamburg, where we would play the two German teams, to inspect the training facilities at Ochsenzoll, a suburb of Hamburg and the base for Bundesliga club, SV Hamburg. What a set-up, a real eye-opener. It had 10 fields, sauna and spa facilities, a medical centre, television room and restaurant. From Hamburg we flew to Berlin, where we would play Chile in the final match of the preliminary round, to look over more training facilities and accommodation.

It was then off to Switzerland for more reconnaissance for a set-up to use before we got to Germany for the start of the finals. I took a liking to the Baeren Hotel in a little town called Birr, near Zug.

It was exactly what I wanted, peaceful and serene, and would allow us to work with very few interruptions.

The entire hotel was booked exclusively for the touring party. This included the 22 players, myself, Scheinflug, tour leader Tom Grimson, manager John Barclay, physio Peter Van Ryn, doctor Brian Corrigan and psychologist John Burgess. Ray Baartz would later be added to that group after tragically being forced to miss the finals because of a serious injury sustained in a lead-up match against Uruguay.

The hotel in Switzerland would also cause me severe problems with Australian officialdom. But more of that later.

A day later we flew to Vienna for a meeting with the Austrian Football Organisation general secretary and his delegation and met at the famous Hotel Zaher for a traditional Austrian lunch. Well, I was again embarrassed by the behaviour of our officials.

This time Le Fevre and Patrick turned up wearing skivvies and leather jackets. I could see the AFO boss was uncomfortable. 'I am sorry, gentlemen,' he said. 'You cannot enter this establishment without a shirt, tie and jacket.' Eventually, someone rounded up the necessary attire.

I have always adhered to the old adage of 'when in Rome, do as the Romans do'. So if a country or federation had something traditional, like a drink or particular food, at a function I would always partake. But Brian and Tom refused the AFO boss's toast of schnapps instead asking for a beer. Even when some of the best wine of the region was offered, they still insisted on drinking beer. I shuddered at their lack of class and etiquette.

It didn't help that later in the day Brian dug in to his pocket to hand out pins to the dignitaries. At the same time, he pricked himself and let out an almighty scream. The pins looked like a toy from a $2 op shop when compared to the elegant and beautifully presented badge and pennant from the AFO. Again our country had been shown up for its crassness.

Finally, we got down to the business of organising a friendly game for the Socceroos only to be shown a three-year schedule of games for the Austrian A, B and C teams. How naïve of us. It made us realise just how small a player we really were in the world game.

Next stop was Budapest, the capital of Hungary, where we met with Secretary General Sandor Berzi at the famous offices of the Hungarian Football Federation. We took an interpreter with us because we understood communication would be very difficult.

Just walking through the rooms was awe inspiring. It was a place steeped in so much football history and tradition. I could feel the hairs on the back of the neck rising. The collection of history was mind blowing.

Again Brian did not endear himself to me. Berzi made a lovely speech congratulating Australia on making the World Cup finals and saying what a wonderful achievement it was when you considered that the likes of Hungary, England, Austria, Czechoslovakia and Romania hadn't.

Instead of replying with dignity, Brian simply said, 'Thanks. We are here to organise some friendlies before the World Cup.' Brian did not appreciate it, but I stepped in immediately and expressed our deepest feeling and respect for being allowed to step through the corridors of one of the great football organisations in the world. We needed games and we needed to butter people up.

Unfortunately, like Austria, the Hungarian national team was already committed to a playing schedule that stretched over the next five years. However, Berzi came up to me later and whispered, 'Whatever you need about East and West Germany, we will provide for you.'

Back at the hotel, Brian said, 'Let's leave this place as quickly as we can.' I asked why. 'Because no-one speaks a word of English,' he said. You could have knocked me over and I could not help myself by replying, 'Excuse me Brian, but do you speak a word of Hungarian?'

We had more luck in Israel, where we arranged two games though, in the meantime, my contact in Switzerland had managed to arrange matches against club sides St Gallen, coached by Zeljko Perusic, Young Boys and Xamax Neuchatal, coached by Lav Mantula. Perusic and Mantula were both well known to me and were a great help with our preparation.

Chapter 11

The Day I Lost My Temper and My Job

I have always considered myself a cool and calm person whether I am in my special little world of coaching or in the normal, everyday environs of life. It takes a hell of a lot to get me angry enough to blow my top or do something irrational.

I would have had every right to do so when we were down 2–0 in the second leg World Cup qualifier against Iran in Tehran in 1973 and looking in all sorts of trouble. Our World Cup dream was being shattered before my eyes but, I was smart enough to realise a cool head and some quick thinking was needed. We managed to keep the score to 2–0 and thus qualified for the next stage 3–2 on aggregate.

Unfortunately, and I am not proud of it, that calmness and steadiness deserted me for one of the very few times in my life on ANZAC Day 1974 in the dressing rooms at Olympic Park in Melbourne.

It is a day etched in my memory forever. Little did I know it at the time, but it was the straw that broke the camel's back in terms of my career as national team coach of Australia.

I have always said, and I think every coach in any sphere of sport—and at any level—would agree, the easiest part of what you do is preparing and selecting the team.

But officialdom and the ego-driven petty politics that goes with it...how do you overcome those obstacles when all you should worry about is football and your players?

I came face to face with my worst nightmare after the Socceroos drew 0–0 with two-times world champions Uruguay in Melbourne. It shouldn't have been that way. I had been delighted with the result against the South Americans as I feared the possibility of the team crumbling and having to face the huge task of rebuilding their confidence before the World Cup finals in West Germany in 1974.

But the boys were superb and showed what they were capable of against a quality side. This was a huge morale booster and we were to get an even better one several days later when we played the Uruguayans in that fateful second match at the Sydney Cricket Ground.

Not surprisingly, our dressing room at Olympic Park was overflowing with well-wishers and backslappers after the Melbourne game. Arthur George walked into the room with Bob Hawke, the then president of the ACTU and future prime minister of our country.

A beaming Arthur came over and tapped me on the shoulder then whispered in my ear, 'I need the names of the 22 players who are going to the World Cup.' To this day I don't know why he was so insistent.

I had already submitted a list of 27 players, which I would reduce to the final number later, to the Federation. I told him that. But he persisted, 'I need the 22 names.' Being just as pigheaded, I fired back again, 'I've submitted 27'.

By this time Arthur was very frustrated and angry. You always knew when he was agitated because he used to have these nervous, funny twitches of the face and would squint his eyes. It always gave the impression that he was smiling. He wasn't. I could see the steam coming out of his ears.

He was in no mood to muck around and said, 'I employ you. I demand 22 names.' Well, enough was enough for me. To this day I still don't know what got over me. It seemed like a red mist descended over me and I did something I guess I have regretted ever since.

I lunged at Arthur, grabbed him around the neck, pushed him towards the dressing room doors and told him to get out. A hush came over the room for several seconds before it turned into uproar. The room exploded as the players stood up on the benches and clapped and cheered. They loved it. They were chanting, 'out, out, out'.

Can you imagine it? The boss of the Federation being treated like that—and in front of dignitaries. Arthur was a smallish man, but he must have felt six inches tall as he disappeared out of the room, yelling out to me, 'I will sack you!' I just wonder what Bob Hawke must have thought.

Of course, I got the last word in by saying, 'Yes, but if you do it now, the country will lynch you!' It was a nice piece of bravado on my part. But with Arthur now out of the room, I turned to the players and said with a smile, 'Thanks. You just got me sacked.'

I was under no illusions about where I stood with Arthur once we got back to Sydney for the second game. To be honest, I felt sorry for him for one of the very few times after what happened in Melbourne. When all was said and done, he was the boss and should have been treated with a little more respect.

Anyway, I decided to telephone him. 'Arthur, Rale,' I said. When he heard who was on the other end of the line, he replied, 'When

I tell you to do something, you do it' before slamming down the receiver. Arthur George was in no mood to be forgiving.

Many people believe it was the Melbourne incident that led to me not being reappointed Socceroos boss for the 1978 campaign after taking the team to the World Cup. Yes, it did not help, but it was only a small part of the overall picture.

Looking back now, I can safely say there were probably four crucial situations which led to my eventual downfall.

The first was my support for the election of Labor leader, Gough Whitlam, as prime minister in 1972. The second was the drama over the squad size.

The third was the role of Englishman, Eric Worthington, and finally my involvement in a Socceroos pay dispute before the World Cup finals. They all added up.

The Whitlam matter probably started it all off. I remember there was a huge push for Gough, who was to become a great friend to me, and still is, to become Prime Minister. He was sweeping the country on the 'It's Time' (for a change of government) theme. There were a host of television, media celebrities and academics supporting him and I was asked to join the list.

I had never been a member of a political party, and I wasn't then and haven't been since. But I had met Gough many times and I liked him. I liked his stature, his sense of humour, his intelligence and his vision.

Gough was, and still is, an amazing individual and I can understand why he is held in such awe and esteem. He has incredible global knowledge and his mind is tremendous. He was also loyal and is fantastic and stimulating company.

I remember when, during my time as coach of Adelaide City in the National Soccer League, he was visiting Adelaide and rang me up from a hotel in town. He invited me over for a beer and a chat. I can't remember what we talked about but I know there would have been no pretence or talking down on his part. He treated people on the same level, no matter what walk of life.

Anyway, I attended a huge Opera House function, which was on national television, and Arthur George, a staunch Liberal, saw it and spotted me. Later that day I went to his offices in Macquarie Street in the city for a scheduled meeting.

As I entered his office he pointed his finger at me and said, 'Never do that again.' I knew what he was talking about, but I played dumb and let him ramble on before we entered into a very serious discussion. For the first time, I ended up pointing my finger at him and told him to mind his own business and never to talk to me about politics or religion. It was more bravado on my part, but it was also just adding fuel to the roaring blaze.

It was all downhill from then on between Arthur, who I thought was a very clever and wily politician, and me.

I think my fate was sealed when Eric Worthington waltzed into Australian soccer in 1973. Before 1972, I had had a terrific relationship with Arthur. In fact, I would say we were on very good terms. I liked his drive. I liked that he listened to me in terms of what was needed for the national team. Money and preparation were never a problem. He agreed to everything I wanted from top class hotels to staff.

When I was made national team coach he said to me, 'I don't know much about soccer. Do what you have to do, just let me know what you are doing.'

It was simple, honest advice.

In my opinion, Worthington poisoned the relationship between Arthur and me and influenced him to get me sacked after the World Cup in 1974. He was always in Arthur's ear about this and that. Criticising the Socceroos' style of play and telling him that our football was too defensive. Arthur was taken in by Worthington's smooth talking and glibness.

In my opinion, Worthington was a nobody, an Englishman who thought he knew everything about the game but, in reality, knew stuff-all. He was made director of coaching, a position that was part funded by cigarette company, Rothmans.

I felt all Worthington was interested in was playing golf and reducing his handicap.

I couldn't fathom how this no-name could suddenly have so much influence in Australian soccer.

What really angered me was the time, in the mid 1980s, when Worthington criticised Frank Arok and me and made explosive and offensive remarks about our accents. What he was saying was that the players were hard-pressed understanding us, and that we did not present a suitable look in regards to the press, especially the electronic media.

From memory, I think the media went to town on that and I remember that my good friend Ray Gatt, who was with the *Sydney Morning Herald* at the time, wrote a huge story. I don't think Worthington realised just how well Frank and I got on with the soccer writers! He also forgot one, simple thing about football...it speaks all languages.

He also knew so little about Frank and me that he did not know we were multi-lingual. Can you imagine Worthington ordering a cup of cha in Red Square in Moscow!

Even today I get angry when I recall Worthington's stupid and ill-founded comments and, I suspect, he still regrets it. I remember he came to visit me while I was coaching Apia Leichhardt in 1987 and tried to apologise by saying his comments had been taken out of context. I listened, but brushed him off. If he wasn't man enough to stand by what he says or thinks then he did not deserve recognition.

I wonder what Worthington would say about the huge infiltration of foreign coaches in various competitions around the world these days. I wonder what he thinks when he looks at the likes of Jose Mourinho (Chelsea), Rafael Benitez (Liverpool), Arsene Wenger (Arsenal) and Gerard Houllier (formerly Liverpool) who are coaching or have coached in the English Premier League. I am sure the last time I listened to these guys they did not have Yorkshire, Lancashire or Cockney accents!

And what about the likes of Brazilians Mario Zagallo and Carlos Alberto Parreira, who have coached in the oil-rich nations like Saudi Arabia, Qatar and Kuwait? What did the Dutchman Guus Hiddink do for South Korea and Phiippe Troussier for Japan in the 2002 World Cup finals? Finally, who is the coach of England? Sweden's Sven-Goran Eriksson.

While Worthington was a quietly spoken person and a good academic, he knew his way around the politics of Australian soccer. He invariably got what he wanted from Arthur George.

Worthington somehow convinced Arthur that the future of coaching in Australia rested with young and what I dubbed junior English coaches.

These guys were usually in their mid-twenties with little or no reputable playing experience and virtually no time to gain any coaching experience.

We had a string of English coaches at various levels such as Brian Green, Jimmy Shoulder, Ron Smith, Dennis Ford and Ron Tindell, who was a very reputable academic and fine player and someone I held in high regard.

But by and large, they have been huge failures. Green took over from me and lasted just a few months before leaving the country in disgrace after an incident in a shopping centre. Jimmy Shoulder was next, leading us to a disastrous World Cup qualifying campaign in 1977. He was rewarded by being appointed head of soccer at the Australian Institute of Sport!

Ron Smith eventually took charge of the AIS and spent many

years there before moving to Asia where he coached at club level for a lengthy period of time. He is now back in Australia and involved with Football Federation Australia as a technical advisor to the Socceroos. One journalist even suggested he should be the FFA's director of coaching.

What has the man done to deserve such an exalted position in Australian soccer? Surely there are more qualified people here and around the world capable of filling Smith's position. I don't think coaching in Asia qualifies you for such a position and I find the situation simply amazing and beyond comprehension.

For me, Arthur George's contribution to Australian soccer is best summed up in his own words uttered at his farewell as ASF chairman at a function at Sydney's Hilton Hotel in the late 1980s. I remember the words vividly, 'When I took over 20 years ago, you were bankrupt. I'm leaving you today and you are still no better off.'

Arthur George was given a standing ovation at the end of the speech, but I remained firmly seated. Someone at the table asked me why I did not get up and applaud him. 'How can I do that?' I replied. 'Can't you understand? He is telling you he has done nothing for the game.'

I wondered aloud to myself, 'Such mentality deserves what it gets.'

Chapter 12

The Socceroos Arrive on the World Stage

AFTER all the fuss and excitement of the World Cup draw I have to say it was a little bit of a let-down when we arrived back in Australia. I was still on a high and wishing the first game could be played the next day but I had a feeling that the general Australian sporting public and some parts of the media simply did not understand the magnitude of the Socceroos achievement or what lay ahead.

It was a weird feeling for me. But to be honest, I didn't have all that much time to dwell on it because everything now seemed to be moving at lightning speed. So much to do, so much to organise and plan.

It wasn't long before Hungarian club side Ferencvaros landed on our doorstep for a two match series. The Hungarians included the renowned Florian Albert, who had starred for his country at the 1966 World Cup. Sadly, he did not play in the game in Adelaide, which we lost 2–1 or in the 0–0 draw in Sydney and that was a huge disappointment for the fans.

It didn't worry me all that much. I was focused on getting the players used to the system I would use in Germany. I was happy with my back four of Doug Utjesenovic, Peter Wilson, Manfred Schaefer and Col Curran, but the midfield, while settled, was a little ineffective and the strikers were not much better.

Then, against my better judgment, I accepted a match against an Auckland invitational side. We were a disgrace and one critic wrote we played like a bunch of sheilas. That match could have done us so much harm in terms of confidence, but the boys were soon to show they were made of stern stuff.

Renowned South Americans, Uruguay, followed soon after for a two-match series that will go down as one of the most controversial, most remembered and saddest I have ever been involved in. It was also the catalyst for the huge bust-up between me and Arthur George.

Uruguay did not include some of their best players but it was nonetheless a very dangerous opponent and had six players—Luis Garisto, Ruben Corbo, Alberto Cardaccio, Juan Masnik, Denis Milar, Fernando Morena and Walter Mantagazza—who would go on to play in the World Cup finals.

Garisto would become public enemy number one in Australia after a frightening incident in the second match in Sydney that will go down as one of the greatest acts of thuggery I have ever witnessed.

More than 22 000 packed Olympic Park in Melbourne on ANZAC Day for the first match which ended in a 0–0 draw after we dominated three quarters of the game. Typically, the South Americans became frustrated and resorted to rough-house tactics, niggly tackles and sneaky, off-the-ball incidents because things did not go their way. It was a foul, ill-tempered performance on their part and they did not endear themselves to the Socceroos or the public.

For our part, it was a fabulous effort and a real morale booster. Goalkeeper Jack Reilly was wonderful, while Curran was probably our best player on the day. Tactically, we were very mature and I was delighted with the way the players handled the rubbish dished out by the Uruguayans. I probably should have taken a leaf out of my players' book and stayed calm when Arthur George confronted me in the dressing room after the game in that infamous incident which saw me kick him out of the rooms.

But I wasn't the only one who clashed with Arthur that day. After the match Arthur, with a huge cigar in his mouth, came into the dressing rooms and approached an almost spent Curran, who was leaning down undoing his boots. Arthur had apparently had problems getting to the game because of flight delays and he was keen to share his story with Col.

'You wouldn't believe what happened to me,' he said to Col. Well, while Col had had a terrific match, he had a huge task in marking a six-foot-plus Uruguayan, so he was in no mood for frivolity afterwards. Col, who was known as 'Bunny' to his mates and was a tough man from Newcastle with a great sense of humour, reached up, grabbed the cigar from Arthur's hand, threw it to the ground and said, 'I couldn't give two fucks!' Arthur was speechless and just walked away. Can you imagine a player getting away with that today?

The return match in Sydney, 48 hours later in front of 25 708 fans at the famous Sydney Cricket Ground, brought both joy and utter desolation. I will never forget it. One of my memories is standing next to then Prime Minister, Gough Whitlam, with whom I had become friends, during the national anthem.

I noticed Gough had tears streaming down his face. I turned to him and said, 'You hear this national anthem five or six times a day. How come you have these tears?' He replied, 'These moments you have no control over. That's a fascinating feeling and I am proud of it.' I understood. From that day on I get tears in my eyes when I hear *Advance Australia Fair.*

While the South Americans continued with their terrible antics—kicking, punching, screaming obscenities and cynical fouling—we played football and very good football at that. The scoreline did not give a true indication of the way we played. We demolished them 2–0 with Ray Baartz setting the ground alight with a magnificent goal from all of 35 metres and Peter Ollerton scoring the other in a memorable victory against the two-times world champions.

After Baartz scored the first goal he was a marked man. The Uruguayans could not handle him and the only way they knew how to stop him was to get him out of the game any way they could. They did it in the most despicable way imaginable. There was a bit of a set-to 15 minutes after the goal and in the melee, Ray was felled by what I still describe as a karate chop delivered to the back of the neck by Garisto. Garisto was sent off but it was small punishment for a bastard of an act.

Ray fell to the ground like a sack of potatoes. He was dazed, stunned. He was semi-conscious, but he managed to get back to his feet. He told me he was fine at half time but I was going to rest him. He refused to go off and completed the game. After the match he started feeling ill. He was given some tablets. It was some 14 hours later that he got very ill and had to be rushed to hospital. I was oblivious to his problems as the team parted ways after the game with the players heading home.

In what was the scariest moment of his life, Ray was partly paralysed. However, he recovered, but it was the end of his football career. It was a shattering blow for Ray and a massive one for Australian soccer.

I regard Baartz as the greatest footballer I have ever dealt with. He is a wonderful character and revered by all the '74 Socceroos.

He has never had an enemy and he is the pride of Newcastle.

Ray was so important to the '74 Socceroos. He was to us what Franz Beckenbauer was to West Germany, what Johan Cruyff was to Holland what Pele was to Brazil and Maradona to Argentina. All of our tactical game was built around him due to his amazing mobility and shooting power. He never played as an out-and-out striker but would come from behind and produce world-class goals.

After the match, as we made our way out of the SCG, Arthur George tried to be funny by introducing me to NSW premier (the late) Sir Robert Askin—he was known as Robin but changed his name by deed poll in 1971—with the words, 'Sir Robert, may I introduce to you the great coach and the greatest son of a bitch.' Quick as a flash, I shook his hand and replied, 'A pleasure meeting another son of a bitch.' He took it in great spirit and had a huge laugh.

In May, I waited until the last 72 hours before the official FIFA deadline to name the 22 players, minus Baartz, who would go to the World Cup. But I demanded Ray came with us. The ASF refused at first, but I would not let the matter rest. Eventually they gave in. I think they feared a terrible backlash from the media and football public if they stopped Ray from going.

At last, we were on our way to Germany. It was May 1974. We left carrying the weight of a nation on our shoulders. Our first stop was Jakarta where we beat Indonesia 2–1 before losing 2–1 to Israel in Jaffa. I missed that game because I went on ahead to Leipzig (East Germany) on a scouting mission with my good friend Peter Stubbe, who I knew from my playing days at Footscray JUST.

Peter was a valuable help to me. He had connections everywhere and his network of scouts provided so much information on both Germanys and Chile. I saw East Germany play England in a 1–1 draw in Leipzig and stayed in the same hotel that Joe

Mercer, then England coach, was staying. Joe was a good man and we spent much time together.

Joe was also a great help and he was a funny man too. Back at the hotel after the game he said to me, 'When you play the East Germans pack the fucking defence and hope for the best. They are robots!'

From Leipzig we headed for Herzogenaurach, the home of Adidas. We collected 210 pairs of brand new boots for the players. The Adidas family was fantastic to us and treated us as one of their own. We conveyed the boots in a Mercedes, provided by Adidas, as we headed to Switzerland to prepare the squad.

The next day we arrived at our exclusive hotel and were soon joined by the players. The media and some ASF officials had also arrived, but they were in for a rude shock because I had booked every room and had instructed the hotel that they were only for the players and staff. For the first time I was not a popular figure with the media. They were unhappy that they would have not as much access to the players as they were used to in the past.

The media had to understand that I had a job to do and I did not want the players to be distracted. We played three games in Switzerland, winning all three though the highlight was watching Brazil play a practice match against FC Basel.

The world champion Brazilians had set up camp in the Black Forest, just across the border in Germany, but they travelled to Basel for the friendly, which had an unusual clause in the contract in that there was to be no tackling whatsoever.

Our players would not miss that match for anything. Brazil was coached by Mario Zagallo and included players such as goalkeeper Leao, Ze Maria, Rivelino, Paulo Cesar, Jairzinho, Luis Pereira, and Valdomiro.

What a performance! Brazil's first goal came from a stunning free kick from Rivelino after the Brazilians had put six players in motion. Rivelino scored again from a free kick 15 minutes later, striking it with the outside of his left foot.

Soon after half-time Rivelino again scored from a free-kick against a goalkeeper who by this stage was a broken and shattered man. I don't know if he ever recovered from that.

During the game Brazil won a corner on the right side. Jairzinho crossed the ball and Rivelino feigned to smash the ball at the defenders. Instead, he transferred the ball to the outside of his left foot and played it to Paulo Cesar. It was fantastic skill from a world class player, but not in the eyes of tour leader, Tom Grimson, who was sitting next to me.

Tom pulled my shirt and said, 'See Rale, even the greatest players in the world make mistakes.' It took all of my control not to fire back at Tom. I said simply and facetiously, 'Yes, Tom.'

We arrived in Hamburg 72 hours before the opening game against East Germany to be treated to typical German efficiency. Everything ran like clockwork from press conferences to training sessions. A vital part of it all was security, which was understandable in light of the 1972 Munich Olympics tragedy. When we arrived at our Ochsenzoll headquarters, there were soldiers stationed every 10 metres. The world, and Germany especially, was still very much on edge. Nothing was being left to chance.

During our stay at Ochsenzoll, we had Uwe Seeler as our liaison officer, though the late Kurt Roessler was our liaison for the entire World Cup campaign in Germany. Seeler was a German national sporting hero, one of the greatest footballers the country has produced.

He was a prolific striker, who played 239 games (137 goals) for Hamburg SV between 1963 and 1972 and played 72 times with 43 goals for his country.

Initially none of the players realised the status of the man. At one stage they were treating him more like a water boy and ball-boy, getting him to fetch them this and that. Something needed to be said. I gathered the players together one day and told them about Seeler. They were stunned. They had not realised. From that point on they treated him with the respect he deserved and the players often asked him for autographs.

Nothing was a problem for the Germans. We were provided with a Mercedes bus for our exclusive use for training and matches while the tour officials had the use of two Mercedes cars with chauffeurs and interpreters.

At this stage, we had not run into too many Australian supporters because we were so secluded, but one incredible man will remain a part of the 1974 family forever. Jim Scane, an Englishman who made his home in Australia, adopted the Socceroos and followed us almost everywhere. He was in Germany and stuck like glue to us. The boys treated him well for they regarded him as family.

Jim is now 90-years-old and has attended almost every reunion, the latest in 2005 before the second leg against Uruguay when he travelled all the way from Cessnock to attend our function in Smithfield, in Sydney's south western suburbs.

He really stood out in Germany, wearing a specially made green and gold suit with matching hat. Every spare inch of the suit and hat was covered in the names of every player in the squad and most of the opponents we played on the way to the World Cup. As each opponent fell by the wayside, he would put a big, red mark across the name. In Germany he had question marks next to the names of East Germany, West Germany and Chile. That suit now hangs proudly in my private Socceroos museum.

We were still flavour of the month with the media and were continually hounded for interviews. One day a media type approached me and asked to speak privately one on one. Incredibly, he wanted me to sign 8000 autographs on a special world-cup stamped envelope and he offered me 8000DM!

I looked at him strangely and the price went up to 12 000 then 16 000. It was too tempting an offer to refuse. The fee exceeded what I had got for coaching the Socceroos for the last four years!

But there was no way I could sign 8000 autographs so I co-opted team psychologist John Burgess to copy my signature. He spent hours practicing. Eventually I signed the first 200 then John signed the rest. I think it took him something like three days! I heard recently that someone in Hanover paid 70 euros for one of the autographs. It would be interesting to find which one he or she got.

While the German media was generally fairly kind to us, some could not resist the temptation to put the boot in and have a laugh at our expense. One newspaper, *Bild Zeitung*, had a story which asked in so many words, 'Why are these kangaroos at the World Cup. Why do we have to put up with this bunch of no-hopers?' It was cruel and lacked integrity, but it was also useful for me as a ploy to stir up the players.

At least that newspaper had the guts to issue an apology after the last match against Chile. They said they were sorry for what they had written and that the Socceroos had been great ambassadors for their country and had performed beyond expectations in the finals.

Out on the practice field, the team was training twice a day and looking good. It is a strange thing to say, but I was feeling quietly confident about the opening game against the East Germans.

As was my custom, I told the players the starting line-up before we left the hotel. It was: Reilly; Utjesenovic, Wilson (captain), Schaefer, Curran; Richards, Mackay, Rooney, Warren, Alston, Buljevic. Curran had been under an injury cloud but was fit. You would have had to hit him with two axes to stop him playing and I decided that John Warren would replace the injured Baartz.

With a police escort, we got to the ground 90 minutes before the match. The players had time to soak up the atmosphere of a World Cup. But it was a different story in the dressing room before kick-off. The players were naturally tense and surprisingly very quiet.

The culmination of four years of hard work, pain, torture, family and work sacrifices, controversy, drama and blood, sweat and tears walked on to the Volksparkstadion in Hamburg in front of about 17 000 fans on June 14 1974. Eleven very proud Australians ready for the fight of their lives.

Every football fan and critic in the world was certain we would be smashed all over the park. Predictions of six and seven goals abounded in the media. The media were doing my work for me yet again! I didn't have to say much to the players. They knew they wouldn't win the World Cup but they knew they had that special something that would not let them down and would drive them to play as they have never played before.

We were prepared for the East Germans. As a methodical, predictable side I considered they would be easier to play against than say a Brazil, a team with flair and individual brilliance. Half the time you did not know what the South Americans would do or come up with. Not so East Germany.

The Germans came out at a furious pace, trying to intimidate us and blast this group of men they believed did not deserve to be on the same park as them to oblivion. They wanted to teach us a lesson. You could see it in their demeanour and you could see it in the way they strutted around the field with and without the ball.

But they were not strutting too much as they walked to the dressing rooms at half-time to a chorus of jeers from the crowd, most of which had started to support the boys from 'kangaroo land'. It was a tremendous half of football from us. Wilson and Schaefer were towers of strength in defence and we caused some problems up front as well. All up we created three good scoring chances. At 0–0, I was feeling extraordinarily calm.

Half-time came at a good time for us, or so I thought. I didn't say all that much to the players. We were fortunate to get away with the off-side trap a number of times, but I wasn't silly enough to expect our luck to hold out in that regard. I pointed to Wilson and said, 'Don't do it (play the off-side trap) again.'

Disaster struck in the 58th minute when Peter tried to play off-side again. He hesitated for a fraction, Curran stayed back a little, Schaefer had committed himself in a tackle and we stopped for the referee's whistle to signal a clear off-side. It didn't come. Suddenly, we were exposed. A quick cross from the left landed in our area. Goalkeeper Jack Reilly came out as a shot came in, the ball deflected towards goal and Curran, charging in at 100mph, only managed to get a foot to it and put it in our own net. It was a heart-breaking own goal, though Curran really couldn't be blamed as the ball was going in anyway.

Instead of dropping their heads, the players lifted but it was all over just 10 minutes later when Streich scored. The final scoreline of 2–0 was a fantastic result, but we could have finished with a draw. We were no pushover and the Germans were glad to see the back of us.

The headlines the next day told the story. I liked the one that said, 'Dwarves grow 10 feet tall!' The stories were all along the same lines, praising Australia and telling how East Germany narrowly avoided being disgraced.

East German coach, Georg Buschner, was highly complimentary of the Socceroos, saying we were very well organised, hard but fair and predicted we would not be on the wrong end of a hiding in the last two matches.

Despite the taste of defeat, the players were in a buoyant mood as they prepared for the second, and easily our hardest match, against West Germany three days later in the same stadium.

This was going to be an awesome task for us for they were a magical side with some of the biggest names in world football such as Gerd Muller, Wolfgang Overath, Beckenbauer, Sepp Maier, Berti Vogts, who coached Scotland recently, Paul Breitner and Uli Hoeness. They were coached by the legendary Helmet Schoen, who coached the national team in four successive World Cups (1966, 1970, 1974 and 1978).

I made just one change to the starting line-up, dropping John Warren and bringing in Ernie Campbell. John had picked up an injury and had been ineffective against East Germany. After that match he did not take part in our final two matches. John had done a wonderful job to come back from a crippling injury. He was held in such high esteem in Australia. He was not the same damaging player after his injury but I had rewarded his courage and determination by selecting him in the 22-man squad, as I had promised him, and I went one further by playing him in the first game. He deserved it. But now was not the time for sentiment.

Before the game Schaefer, who was born in Germany and had received unprecedented coverage in the media during the finals, was keyed up to mark the exceptional striker Muller, who had been a sensation at the 1970 World Cup when he finished as leading goalscorer.

This was the biggest moment in Manfred's career. I remember him being quoted, 'I have been preparing for this for a long, long time. I am ready for the biggest 90-minute duel of my career. If I can keep Muller scoreless it will be the greatest achievement of my career.'

It wasn't to be. In front of a sold-out stadium of 70 000, Muller scored with a back header in the 53rd minute as West Germany recorded a 3–0 win after a piledriver of a shot from Wolfgang Overath and a 35th minute strike from Bernhard Cullman. But the scoreline did not do us justice.

V for victory. Very happy after the Socceroos won the first stage World Cup qualifiers in 1973.

Top: Job done. Chaired off by Ray Richards, Jim Fraser and Jim Mills after the great win against South Korea. Goal scorer Jim Mackay (far right) is well pleased.

Bottom: A toast. Socceroos captain Peter Wilson and I share a glass of champagne in Sydney airport after the win over South Korea in Hong Kong.

Top left: That's my boy. With my son Simon (aged two) before heading off for the World Cup finals in 1974.

Top right: On guard. Sharing a joke with an armed guard during training in Germany.

Bottom: The greatest—meeting Brazilian legend Pele at the 1974 World Cup in Germany.

Top left: The first one. Showing off the NSL coach of the year award in 1977.

Top right: German great. Sharing a glass of wine with the Kaiser—German legend Franz Beckenbauer during the visit of New York Cosmos to Australia.

Bottom: What a player. Scottish great Dixie Deans in action for Adelaide City during my stint at the club. A fearsome player, he had a weakness—spiders.

Top: I had the pleasure of meeting the late Reggae singer Bob Marley during his visit to Adelaide in 1980.

Bottom: Who's that man next to Rale Rasic? Here I am holding the NSL champions cup after winning the title with Apia-Leichhardt. Australian Prime Minister Bob Hawke is on my right while Apia chairman Joe Preztia admires the silverware.

Top: Here's cheers. Celebrating after winning the National League title with Apia-Leichhardt in 1987. Apia official Ron Orsatti is on my left. His son Andrew works for SBS TV.

Bottom: You are the one. Former England, Liverpool and Hamburg star Kevin Keegan during one of our coaching clinics in Australia.

A great moment. Lighting the flame after carrying the Olympic torch at Narooma in 2000.

Top: Australian boxing legend Johnny Famechon and myself at a Sport Australia Hall of Fame function.

Bottom: Growing old gracefully. The 1974 team at a 30-year reunion in Sydney in 2004.

It was in this game that we twice came very close to scoring our first goal in the World Cup finals. First Alston caused a sensation when he glided past Beckenbauer then George Schwarzenbeck before shooting in to the arms of Maier. I had brought on Atti Abonyi for Campbell and Peter Ollerton for Buljevic at half-time and Atti went within an inch of scoring when he collected a pass from Jimmy Mackay and struck a fine shot, only to see it hit the post.

The local fans were baying for blood after the third goal and they expected a rout. It didn't come and, incredibly, there were jeers for the German side and cheers for the Socceroos every time we touched the ball. It was there and then that Australian soccer arrived on the world stage.

Not surprisingly, the media heaped more praise on the Socceroos. They were filling pages with stories of what football was like back home, of how the players were semi-professionals and worked day jobs to earn enough money to live on. It was extraordinary stuff and the German public and media lapped it up. They could not get enough of it.

After that wonderful effort against the eventual world champions, who went on to beat Holland 2–1 in the final, I gave the boys the night off to go out on the town and I didn't really expect to see them till the early hours of the next morning even though I had given them a curfew. But would you believe, every one of them was back long before the time I had set. The rugby league, rugby union and AFL stars of today could learn about professionalism from these men.

The next day we travelled to Berlin and set camp in a luxury hotel to prepare for our final match against Chile in the Olympiastadion which is the home of Bundesliga club, Hertha Berlin, and had been made famous during the 1936 Olympic Games after Adolf Hitler had allegedly refused to shake hands with American superstar athlete, Jessie Owens, because he was black. Owens had won four gold medals inside that stadium.

The reason I chose the luxury of a hotel was because I did not want the players to be caught up in the regimented atmosphere we had to endure in Hamburg. They needed some space and some extra care. It was a reward for the players who had given so much, not only in the first two matches but over the last four years. They deserved it.

We saw the game against Chile as our chance to achieve something remarkable. The entire squad was full of confidence. We had stretched East and West Germany to the limit, so why couldn't we go one better against Chile?

The South Americans, however, would not be a pushover. They had finished third at the 1962 World Cup and boasted a fine array of players who possessed that typical South American flair and unpredictability. In Elias Figueroa, Carlos Humberto Caszley and Alberto Quintano, the Chileans had some very recognisable world players.

I had done a lot of work on Chile but I still insisted on dispatching Eric Worthington, who had not been long in the job of the ASF's director of coaching after coming from England, to Berlin to watch them play East Germany. And what did I get back? No written report, though I was told, 'Chile is nothing much except they have two big lads at the back.' This was fantastic information for a coach to prepare tactics. And you wonder why I am so critical of officialdom!

The Chile match was an incredible affair. There had been demonstrations before the game started by people protesting against the dictatorial rule of the Chilean government. When the game kicked off in front of 16 000 fans it was dry but cloudy. The heavens opened up soon after and the ground was almost awash. It was a mini lake.

The Chileans were desperate to win this game. It was a matter of honour for them. They could not be beaten by an inferior team like Australia. To give them an added incentive, the Chilean Football Federation offered the players an $8000 bonus each to beat the Socceroos.

The match conditions were dire once the rain came. The second half didn't start for 20 minutes and I had to literally drag the Iranian referee out of the room to get him to re-start the match.

To be honest, the rain was a godsend for us, for the Chileans were playing some superb football and causing us all sorts of problems. When the rain started falling we came into our own. We started to dominate. Mackay had a clear penalty denied while Abonyi and Buljevic also had good chances to score.

The Chileans were getting frustrated, as South American footballers often do when things don't go their way. There was a lot of shirt pulling and niggly fouls and the referee was having a hard time controlling the players.

Then disaster struck. Curran was struggling with injury and I was telling Ray Richards to slow the game down as I had Harry Williams warming up to go on. But it backfired on me. Ray did such a good job of delaying things that the referee sent him off. Ray now had the dubious honour of being the first and only Australian to be sent off in a World Cup finals match! He hasn't lived it down since.

There was still seven minutes to go. Chile was coming home strongly and we were under enormous pressure. My heart almost stopped beating with a minute to go when a high cross from Figeuroa slipped through Jack Reilly's fingers and was heading for the goal until Peter Wilson headed it clear.

The 0–0 draw with a very good side that had drawn with East Germany and had lost only 1–0 to West Germany was a huge result for Australian soccer. It was our first point at the finals.

Hopefully, it won't be our last with the 2006 Socceroos ready to show the world that Australian soccer has returned to the world scene.

After the match, the team showered, boarded the bus and went back to the hotel for a meal together. But before dinner I called the players together for a private meeting.

I thanked them for everything they had done for their country, themselves and family, and for me. I would have been nothing except for them. I thanked them for their sacrifices, both family and work-wise. They had bled for their country and their mates, and they had done themselves proud.

After four years living in each other's pockets, it took me just six minutes to end my association with the team. I knew what was coming my way. The next day the headlines in the newspapers back home told the story. Arthur George had been quoted as saying I would not be re-appointed as national coach.

Sadly, it was now the end of an era. The campaign marked the end of the international careers of a number of great servants to the game. It was a long and distinguished list—Schaefer, Richards, Warren, Curran, Watkiss, Tolson, Campbell, Buljevic, Milisaljevic, Gary Manuel, Ivo Rudic, Mackay, Fraser and Baartz.

Mackay went on to play two more games for Australia before retiring. It was one of the saddest days in my life when Jimmy passed away after suffering a heart attack in the late 1990s. The first of the 1974 Socceroos family had left us. However, I have always made it a point to stay in touch with his son, Malcolm, who is like a son to all of us. Malcolm, who lives in New Zealand, regularly attends our re-unions, no matter where they are held.

John Warren's death, from cancer, in 2004 also hit us hard. He had fought a brave battle, as you would expect from a man of his character. When he passed away in hospital, Ray Richards and John Watkiss were by his bedside. Ray took it hard.

After the final whistle against Chile, there was a huge sense of relief that this incredible four-year journey had come to an end. I was mentally drained. Almost every spare minute of my waking hours during those four years had been devoted to the Socceroos. The rewards were truly fantastic, a blessing. But now it was over.

There were muted celebrations after the match against Chile. Players went their own way. I guess they had seen enough of each other. After dinner a few went into town, others visited clubs, some just stayed in the hotel to soak up the last remnants of what was the greatest moment of their football careers.

The squad eventually returned to Australia but I stayed behind in Germany to fulfil some media commitments writing reports for, incredibly, the same newspaper that had taken the mickey out of the team a week earlier, *Bild Zeitung*. It was probably best I stayed behind for I have no doubt that had I returned with the squad I would have been involved in a full-blown clash with Arthur George.

In the end, I just didn't want anything to be taken away from the squad. The 1974 Socceroos had achieved untold success. We were trailblazers, the undisputed champions of Asia and Oceania. We had remarkable results against world class opposition and we qualified for the World Cup. You could not have asked for more.

This Yugoslav orphan who had been taken into the hearts of the Australian sporting public felt incredibly privileged to be part of it all. I also made many, many friends and almost as many enemies, but there were no regrets, not one little bit.

Unfortunately, it took another 31 years before Australia was to qualify for the World Cup finals again. How ironic that when Australia beat Uruguay in a penalty shoot-out at Telstra Stadium in November 2005, it meant the Socceroos would return to the scene of their greatest moments, Germany, for the World Cup.

Who said lightning doesn't strike in the same place twice?

Chapter 13

From Hero to Zero—My Biggest Kick in the Stomach

FOOTBALL has been my life and my passion. It has given me untold success, pleasure and happiness. I am indebted to the game and I always will be.

But as with anything in life, there are times when you wonder why you bothered and you question whether it has been worthwhile or not. The path can be littered with pot holes and barriers and you learn to take the good with the bad. Needless to say, the sport has also been the source of some of the darker moments in my life.

Probably the two biggest kicks in the guts I ever got were my sacking as Socceroos coach following the 1974 World Cup finals at the age of 38 and the 1993 Stewart Inquiry into the transfer of local talent overseas.

It is difficult to say which one troubled me most, except that both events had a marked effect on me and my family and taught me much more about the business of dirty politics that has infested and just about destroyed Australian soccer over the years. These days I look back on those two quite disturbing events and wonder how I kept my sanity. My dumping as coach of the Australian side was a bitter pill to swallow. And yes, it still hurts when I think about it these days!

The Stewart Inquiry was a fiasco, an embarrassment, an insult and it hurt me deeply. I still get angry when I think about what my family and I went through because of the viciousness of some people and the downright lies they told.

But first the Socceroos job.

I had dedicated four years to the national team and helped bring the success our football nation had been crying out for—World Cup qualification—and to suffer the terrible treatment I received at the hands of officials will remain with me forever.

Instead of being lauded for the greatest achievement in the history of our sport, I was pilloried, publicly humiliated and made to feel an outcast by these people. It would not have happened anywhere else in the civilised world.

During my reign, the Socceroos went from a nondescript, poorly paid, tin-pot rabble forced to put up with fifth-rate training pitches and hotels and lucky to get a sandwich for lunch to being as close as you can get to a professional organisation and to one of the most revered sporting teams this country has ever produced.

Along with the players, I was so proud of what we achieved for the game here and, rather naively perhaps, I thought it would count for something in the long run. Sadly, I was wrong...very, very wrong.

The writing, I guess, was on the wall as far as my future was concerned when the far from publicity shy Arthur George held court, as he so often liked to do, with the Australian media after our 0–0 draw with Chile in our last World Cup match.

He told them in no uncertain terms that I was finished. I would no longer be the coach. And he repeated those statements on his return to Australia. Revenge was going to be his and he was going to get his way, no matter the cost.

In the end, I had had one too many ding dongs with Arthur. It had been a constant, draining, demanding, mind-numbing battle on a number of fronts with him and his so-called advisors over the four years...from the quality of training grounds, to accommodation, to warm-up games, to outside interference, to player payments, and on and on and on.

I stood up for what I believed and for what I wanted. And I did not budge, not one inch, until I got what I wanted for the team. He didn't like that. He refused to accept it.

I also did not endear myself to some people in high places when I made noises about being paid only half the bonus money I was promised for making the finals. The ASF denied this and I learned a lesson. The ASF did not have anything in writing about the bonus money and I was accused of being the ring leader in stirring up the players through the media. Still, I wanted to stay as coach and Arthur told me I would be the front-runner for the Socceroos job again. But things soured again soon after I was asked, and declined, to act as an advisor to the national team in 1975.

Director of coaching, Eric Worthington, was put in charge of the Socceroos for games against Legia Warsaw before Victorian Tony Boggi took charge for matches against Glasgow Rangers, China, Manchester United and Benfica.

Eventually, Englishman Brian Green was appointed, on advice from Worthington, as fulltime Australian coach.

He lasted a few games before he left Australia under amazing circumstances after being caught for shoplifting two LP records. He was charged and convicted and eventually resigned as national coach and returned to England in March 1976.

Despite the 1974 success and the dramas surrounding Green, Arthur, who was clueless about football and was having his buttons pushed by a group of people I called the Pommy Mafia, was intent on securing an overseas English coach for the national team.

Let me make it clear here that I have nothing against English people because some of my best mates are English, Scottish or Irish and one or two have labelled me McRasic. Some of my good mates include the likes of former players Frank Haffey, Willie Ormond, Tommy Gemmell (who scored for Celtic in the 1967 European Cup final victory), Willie Wallace (who also played in that game), Ray Clemence, Kevin Keegan, Graeme Souness and Tommy Docherty. Look at the quality of these people.

The Australian Soccer Federation eventually placed an advertisement in 1976, looking for a big name to come into the picture. The big name was supposed to be Englishman Alan Vest. He was earmarked for the job by Eric Worthington.

Vest went on to coach Newcastle in the National League and has since coached in Asia. He is now involved at Perth Glory as an assistant coach. By this time I had been offered a job as technical director and national coach of Hong Kong. It was very tempting, but Arthur convinced me I would get the Australian job again and to be patient. 'Don't be silly...just be patient,' he said to me. It is one of the greatest regrets in my life, but I turned down the Hong Kong offer. Duped again!

While I retained hope, I think I knew deep down in my heart that I had no chance of getting the Australian job. I still went ahead and applied, as did Johnny Warren.

Despite the controversy over the Socceroos captaincy issue when I elected to retain Peter Wilson over John for the World Cup finals, John and I were on good terms.

We consulted each other regarding the Socceroos coaching position and came to a pact: John suggested if he got the job he would assume the role of technical director and I would be the coach. If I got the job I would ensure John had a role with the team.

Eventually John and I made it to the interview process, leading to a comical, crazy, embarrassing and incredible sequence of events so typical of Australian soccer.

I'll never forget that day at the old McLeay Travelodge in Kings Cross in Sydney late in 1976. How apt that the meeting was held in this part of the town, a seedy haven for prostitutes. The setting fitted the occasion for the game was to again be prostituted by the subsequent events at that meeting.

John and I sat outside waiting our turn to be interviewed by a panel that included Arthur, Brian Le Fevre, the late Vic Tuting (Tasmanian delegate), Karol Rodny (NSW power broker), Ian Brusasco (Queensland delegate who also went on to become ASF chairman in the late 1980s), the late Sam Papasavas (former NSL chairman), Michael Weinstein (from Victoria), Tony Palumbo (from NSW and now a commentator with SBS) and delegates from Western Australia and South Australia, whose names I can't remember and probably a couple more nondescripts.

The minute I walked into that room I knew my fate was sealed, even though I had been told John and I would get the support of NSW and Victoria. I could sense it in the air. Some of them, Arthur's supporters, could barely look me in the eye. Their minds had been made up.

Brusasco started off by asking me if I would be prepared to give away playing defensive football. It was a set-up question for sure, designed to get me to react. It did the job and I reacted like a bull to a red rag! I took a pen and threw it at Brusasco and said, 'Explain to me the difference between attacking and defensive soccer.'

With that, I stood up slowly and asked, 'Are there any more questions for me gentlemen?' No-one said anything and I walked out of that room. The whole thing lasted all of three minutes. I walked out laughing and when John saw me he cried out, 'Jesus!' He could not believe the interview had been so short.

John was a nervous character at the best of times and I could see he was on the edge. I told him what had happened and all he could say was, 'Fucking bastards'.

The incredible thing is that John's interview lasted less than mine! The first and only question he got was from the WA delegate, 'Tell us about yourself?' Yes, that's right, one of the greatest players we have ever produced was asked to tell this official what he had done in the sport. Amazing.

When John walked out of that room his face was glowing, it was as red as a beetroot. All he could say was, 'Fucking bastards' over and over again. By this time we were both so worked up we went for a drink. John downed two straight scotches in two minutes. I had never seen him like that.

The story doesn't finish there, however. What eventually happened at that meeting will go down as possibly the greatest debacle in our game's history. I'll let Tony Palumbo, who was a NSW delegate at the meeting, take up the story.

'The full executive of the Australian Soccer Federation met that day to interview the four candidates—Rale, John, Alan Vest and Jim Shoulder.

'In those days, NSW and Victoria held 50 per cent of the vote which meant that whoever we voted for could not be beaten. The two organisations had decided before hand that we would vote for Rale and John to do the job together.

'But something was up. During a break following the interviews, Sir Arthur came up to us [NSW and Victorian representatives] and said that he had been thinking long and hard about the voting process and that it would be best that when we voted we would first vote for the person we wanted to eliminate.

'We knew something was up, but we couldn't do anything about it. Rale's name came up first and the other states voted as a bloc and he was eliminated. The same thing happened to John Warren.

'At this point Karol Rodny turned to me and Sam Papasavas and asked, 'What are we supposed to do now?

'I replied, "If he [Arthur] wants to turn this into a joke, let it be a joke."

'Sir Arthur would have been smug by now as he would have been sure that his man, Alan Vest, would get the job.

'We voted again then the votes were tallied and a shaken Sir Arthur got up and said, "Gentlemen, you never cease to amaze me...Jimmy Shoulder is the new Australian coach."

'It was at that stage that a delegate turned to Sir Arthur and said, "You have got the coach you deserve."

'NSW and Victoria had turned the tables on Sir Arthur George.'

I remember the subsequent media furore surrounding Shoulder's appointment. Lawrie Schwab wrote that Arthur was fuming after the ballot.

Schwab wrote, 'Shoulder emerged triumphant 17 votes to 7. The least likely candidate, a 29-year-old with little experience as a team coach, was now the Socceroos' supremo. The soccer world was staggered.'

'Sir Arthur was reported to have told the media that Vest would have won the ballot 13–11 had NSW not voted for Shoulder.'

Shoulder went on to lead the Socceroos to a miserable, disastrous World Cup campaign in 1977 and, as Schwab wrote later, 'What a comedown from the glory of 1973–74!'

As for the Stewart Inquiry, make no mistake, it was a farce, a sham, a piece of political expediency. How could you have an inquiry when people were not required to give evidence under oath?

Anyone could have walked off the street and made any sort of allegation and sullied the names of anyone they did not like. People's names were dragged through the mud without a shred of evidence. Reputations were tainted and lives were almost ruined by people driven by jealousy, agendas and vendettas.

In my case, I was accused of using my position as a prominent coach to sell insurance and of asking the parents of one player for a payment to ensure he got into one of the junior national teams.

I was staggered when those accusations were put to me and the shock of it all stayed with me for some time. Now I look back on it and I can have a bit of a laugh.

I can certainly laugh at the accusation that I asked for a $100 000 payment to get a kid into the junior national side. The kid hadn't even played for a national league side. The stupidity of the accusation is that I supposedly asked for $100 000! Ridiculous! Remember, this was supposed to have happened in the early 1990s. No senior, well established player at the time would have been worth even $50 000 let alone some pimply 16-year-old kid who never played in the NSL. The record transfer for a player in the NSL at the time was $40 000 for seasoned campaigner and quality footballer, Michael Reda, when he joined Adelaide City.

As for the insurance matter, I say this. In my long career spanning over 50 years, I have helped coach over one million kids around the world with involvement from people like John Warren, Kevin Keegan, Franz Beckenbauer and Sir Stanley Matthews. I never had one complaint, apart from the one at the Stewart Inquiry. Enough said.

Yet, one complaint was enough to drag my name and my family through the mud. The thing that hurt me was my family being brought into it. One journalist made insinuations regarding my son, Simon, in one of his stories. What an insult. He had never met Simon. He wouldn't have known what Simon was like. These were the sort of depths with which some people went to try and discredit me.

In the end, however, I was vindicated despite Stewart's recommendation for a police inquiry. I'll never forget the day I was called to police headquarters in Surry Hills for what I thought was going to be questioning on the matter as part of the police inquiry. While I had nothing to hide, I was nonetheless very nervous and apprehensive. I need not have worried!

As soon as I walked in the door I was treated like a king. People were smiling and making a terrific fuss and I was asked to sign untold autographs.

I was taken into a room where I signed five soccer balls, four Australian jerseys and all sorts of memorabilia. There was a table laden with food and sweets. It was one of the best days I have ever had.

I asked the superintendent when they were going to question me and was told, 'We have nothing to ask you'. While I was still angry and upset that I had been put through such an ordeal with the Stewart Inquiry, I remember walking out of the police building feeling on top of the world and with some sense of vindication.

As I walked down the street, I reflected on the wonderful support of my family and friends and some members of the media like *The Australian's* Ray Gatt and the *Daily Telegraph's* John Taylor.

Of course, others suffered like my very good friend Les Scheinflug and the late Eddie Thomson, who coached the great Sydney City sides of the 1970s and early 1980s as well as the Socceroos.

Les had a distinguished career as a player and a coach in Australia. He was the Socceroos first World Cup captain. He coached the national team, was coach of the year in the NSL and earned a worldwide reputation as a junior coach with the Joeys and Young Socceroos.

Along with Thomson, Les was embroiled in the Stewart Inquiry and, as a result, Stewart recommended they both be banned for life before a subsequent Senate Inquiry cleared them of all wrongdoing and they were able to resume their careers.

The one thing that has always irked me about the inquiry is the fact that if the authorities thought they had a tight case against anyone, why didn't they publicly release Stewart's findings themselves? The answer is obvious—they would have ended up in court and faced millions of dollars worth of payouts for defamation because they had no evidence. They would have been laughed out of court.

In the end, they had to go to the Australian senate where politicians used 'coward's castle' to make all sorts of unsubstantiated claims without having to provide any evidence. This protected those who originally made the allegations from being sued.

Chapter 14
Coaching, Coaches and Feuds

WHAT makes a good coach?

If I have been asked once, I've been asked ten thousand times over the years. There is no simple answer to that question. Rather it is a combination of factors, a total package. Some people were born to be coaches, others were self-made.

Nothing guarantees you success as a coach. Some of the greatest players in the world turned out to have little success as coaches. Pele, Paolo Rossi, Franco Baresi and Maradona come to mind. Yet many who never made it beyond park football have turned into legendary coaching figures on the world stage. This is not restricted to the world game. It goes across the broad spectrum of sports.

It takes something special to be able to devote your life to a profession that has the ability to cause you so much pain, to crush you with its almost unbearable pressure and to turn your private life upside down. Yet people thrive on it, day in and day out, week in and week out and decades in and decades out.

It is like a drug—once it gets into your system you can't get rid of it. It is in your blood forever. It is a rush, a wild ride through a gamut of emotions but by the same token, it is one of the most satisfying and rewarding experiences imaginable.

But you can't coach without having a natural love, an undeniable passion for your sport. That is the special ingredient for me—being committed to something specific and devoting your time and every ounce of your energy to being as professional as possible, even though it can come at a tremendous personal cost.

Being a football coach, or any sporting coach, at the highest level, can take its toll. The intrusion on your personal life is massive, as many high profile coaches around the world have discovered over the years. Just look at the pressure on England coach Sven-Goran Eriksson and what he has had to go through.

His name is rarely out of the newspapers and his face is splattered all over the television for both professional and personal reasons. Nothing is sacred to the media, especially in England, where some in the press would sacrifice their grandmothers if it meant a scoop.

Thankfully, I have always had a terrific relationship with the media, especially in Australia. I have made great friends among them including Tom Anderson, David Jack, John Taylor, Ray Gatt, Brian Mossop, Roy Masters, David Fordham, Tony Charlton, Frank Pangallo, Bruce McAveney, Neil Jamison and Phil Wilkins. Importantly, they have always respected the boundaries between my career and my family life.

As for my family life, I can't hide from the fact that it suffered because of my work with the Socceroos and at club level. I was family oriented but even when I wasn't coaching I always threw myself into other projects such as guest speaking, various business initiatives and inventions and, of course, junior coaching clinics (both here and overseas) and private one-on-one tuition for select kids. There were many times when I was home physically but, mentally, I was somewhere else. There was always something going on. I questioned myself at times about when it would stop.

I remember one incident that shook me up after arriving back in Sydney from a tour with the Socceroos. Simon, who was only about two at the time, raced over yelling, 'My daddy, my daddy.' The only problem was he was heading straight for journalist Brian Mossop, who had a moustache and looked nothing like me.

It is my greatest regret that I wasn't around for the best part of my children's lives, watching Simon and Daniella growing up and going through the various important stages like birthdays and first schooldays. Unfortunately, I was obsessed by the game; it was like living in your own little world.

You try and make up for it, but you can never recapture it. Still, I am so very proud of Simon and Daniella and my grandchildren, Aimee, Alexandar, Olivia and Malibu. They mean everything to me and there is nothing I wouldn't do for them.

Even now there are days when I am highly emotional when I think about what I missed doing with my family. Would I do it differently if I had the chance? Unequivocally, yes. But sadly, you can't change things. What's done is done.

My commitment with the national team made a mockery of the suggestion that I was a part-time coach of the Socceroos. Yes, there were many times when nothing was happening with the team in terms of camps, matches or tournaments. But my mind was never part-time when it came to coaching the Socceroos. I lived it and breathed it.

I particularly liked the psychological aspect of coaching, to be able to get into the minds of the players, to read their moods, to understand what they are feeling, how they are coping, especially with individual problems like employment and family issues. I was the first to introduce psychology to sport in this country through the late Talbot Smith and that makes me very proud because, at the time, some journalists confused psychology with psychiatry.

Coaching means you have to be a combination of teacher, mentor, psychologist, best mate and confidante. As coach of the Socceroos I like to think I was all of that and more!

I used to spend hour after hour studying players and working out what I could do for them, how I could make them happy and, subsequently, better players. Every player has a different personality trait, something that sets them apart from others.

I always wanted to create a family-type environment with the players where they could come to me to talk one-on-one and have a heart-to-heart maybe during a walk or over coffee. It was a special bond.

That's why you also have to be a brilliant selector because, sometimes, you have to choose the man with reasonable ability ahead of the standout or brilliant player. Someone could be a great player, but unstable as a person.

He is more likely than not to cause problems. I'll take a good player with a great character, a superb sense of humour and an unshakeable will to win over a brilliant but mentally soft player any time.

Two prime examples are Max Tolson, who played an integral part in the 1974 Socceroos and Marshall Soper, one of the most gifted players I have seen and had the pleasure of coaching. What a contrast, however.

Soper had undeniable talent and skills. He had great ball control, vision and the ability to score out of nothing. I will never forget his performance for the Socceroos against the mighty Italian side Juventus in the early 1980s when he tore them apart. The Italians were so frustrated by him that they tried to kick him out of the game.

But for all of his talents, Marshall, who undoubtedly had the talent to play in most leagues around the world at the time, simply did not have the mental strength needed to take him to the very highest level. In my opinion, he could be brilliant one day, but awful the next. You just did not know which Marshall Soper would turn up for a game.

Maxy was a different kettle of fish. What you saw with Maxy, you got. He wasn't a great player by any stretch of the imagination and it would be fair to say Soper had it all over him in terms of ability and out and out skill. But you could never find a more inspirational player, a leader. He would walk through brick walls and fire for his team-mates.

He had this intimidating presence about him. The opposition would only have to look at him once and they would be psyched out. Now you know what I mean when I say I prefer to choose a man ahead of the player.

There is no doubt that, for me, being involved with the Socceroos was, given the incredible make-up of the game in the country, possibly one of the most unique and complex jobs in world football at the time.

It was a huge challenge because of the amazing cultural mix. Don't forget, Australian soccer was an incredible pot pourri of nationalities—German, Yugoslav, Greek, Italian, Maltese, Hungarian, English, German, Scottish and Australian to mention but a few.

Of course, it was different overseas. It was unheard of to have, say, anyone but a German in their national team, anyone but an Italian in their side or anyone but an Englishman in the England team.

But here I was, like a barman, mixing up all these ingredients into an incredible and unique cocktail and turning it into a recipe for success. It was also a potentially explosive make-up because I had to deal with so many cultures, so many traditions. But it came together extraordinarily well.

Even today you still get the likes of the Germans and English sometimes looking down on each other—something perpetuated by the media in both countries—with suspicion and derision in an obvious carry-over from the world wars.

So you can imagine that suspicion was even stronger back in the early 1970s—some 26 years after the end of World War 2—in Australia. I had to make sure than any prejudices and ethnic rivalries were cast aside. The players had to be one and they had to be mates and that included Yugoslavs and Hungarian, Germans and English, Greeks and Macedonians.

It was also very important for me to have great back-up staff and network of coaches, not just local but worldwide. I needed people I could trust and have utmost faith in. Coaching is not a one-man job. Look at all the set-ups, both at club and international level. The coaching staff can number as many as 10, depending on the size of the club or country.

I make no secret of the fact I was heavily influenced by Yugoslav and Hungarian football and the men behind it. There is no doubt that during my time these two countries provided most of the international coaches on both a club and country basis.

Even today, Yugoslav coaches are much sought after all over the world. Look at Bora Milutinovic, who took five teams to the World Cup finals. What a record, what an incredible man. Also, Yugoslavs virtually run Chinese football via the numerous academies and leading clubs.

One of the superstars of coaching is Yugoslav, Ilija Petkovic, who is in charge of the very successful Serbia-Montenegro and has gained a huge reputation for his outstanding work.

Gustav Sebes, Martin Bukovi and Lajos Baroti (all Hungarians), Yugoslavs Lou Brocic (who coached Yugoslavia, Barcelona and Juventus), Branko Zebec (who Franz Beckenbauer once regarded as one of the best coaches in the world), Zlatko Cajkovski (who Gerd Muller regarded as a super coach), Vujadin Boskov (who coached Yugoslavia, Sampdoria and Real Madrid) and Tomislav

Ivic (who coached Hajduk Split and Ajax Amsterdam), Germany's Dettmar Kramer, Poland's Kazimierz Gorski, Englishman Joe Mercer and, finally, Czechoslovakia's Dr. Josef Venglos are the people who influenced and helped me so much in my development in terms of vision, shrewdness and tactical awareness as a club and national team coach.

Then there was Mario Zagallo, who tops my list as an idol and person. The Brazilian maestro has coached all around the world with great success. He won the World Cup as a player and coach. And at 75 years of age his love of football and his thirst and hunger for knowledge has not diminished one little bit.

I will always remember the night in Sydney after the Zagallo-coached Kuwait played the Socceroos in a World Cup qualifier in 1977, which we lost 2–1 under Jimmy Shoulder. Along with Carlos Alberto Parreira and Raul Blanco, I had the pleasure of talking to the great man until four in the morning at the Rushcutters Bay Travelodge.

Another big influence apart from Eastern bloc coaches, was Argentine master, Helenio Herrera, who coached Inter Milan and was known for the system called *catenaccio*. He knew how to close up games once he got in front in very critical situations and I tried to copy that style. Herrera's motto was 'discipline for all'.

Whoever tells you that coaching is not about winning, should look himself in the mirror. I can't recall the name of the club that kept a coach who was losing week in and week out.

I also had a lot to do with the great Scottish coach, Tommy Docherty, possibly one of the greatest characters the world game has seen. Not only was Tom a great coach but he was legendary for his sense of humour and quick and often biting wit. He is also a wonderful human being, kind and gentle with a soft side to his personality that he has rarely shown in public.

Tom developed a love for Australia, coming here as Manchester

United coach when the great club toured in 1975, beating an Australian XI 4–1 in Sydney before returning in the early 1980s to coach Sydney Olympic in the national league.

Prominent NSW and ASF official and life member, Johnny Thompson, a good friend of Docherty's, arranged for me and some players to play a game of foot tennis against Manchester United at Alexandria basketball stadium. Atti Abonyi, Doug Utjesenovic, Ray Baartz, Adrian Alston, John Warren and myself took on the likes of Lou Macari, Sammy McIroy, Steve Coppell and Docherty and we gave them a 42–28 hiding. Tommy was furious and didn't take it too kindly at all. He carried on like he had just lost the World Cup, English championship and FA Cup in one go. He liked to win everything, even a handshake.

But for all of his toughness, there was the soft side and during some of our deep discussions over dinner I saw him cry like a baby several times.

Of course, he was renowned for his humour, though he was taken aback one day when one of his intended jokes fell flat. The great ABC radio and television broadcaster Norman May interviewed Tom one day and to illustrate a point about what it was like to lose a big match, he said to Norman, 'It would bring a tear to a glass eye.'

He did not know Norman indeed had a glass eye and when I told him he went red-faced and let out an almighty 'fucking hell.' Needless to say, Norman took it in great spirit.

Tommy, of course, was a journalist's dream because of the outrageous things he used to say. He was great copy because he did not care on whose toes he would tread. He made a real hit in Australia during Rudi Gutendorf's reign as Socceroos coach in the late 1970s, early 1980s.

He was bewildered by the German's coaching methods and one day he let the media know in no uncertain terms. The next day, one back-page headline screamed, 'Docherty declares, "I'll coach Australia for a dollar!' He didn't, but I wonder what would have happened had he done so. One thing is for certain, his battle with Australian soccer officialdom would have been something to behold.

When you talk of someone being born to coach, I like to use the great Australian Rules masters, Kevin Sheedy and Ron Barassi, as examples. Both are inspirational men and ever-lasting figures in the game on and off the field.

They are always willing and happy to share their experiences and knowledge with anyone who wants to listen. I have had the privilege of knowing both men quite well.

For me, Sheedy is a remarkable man. He has done it all, yet his love of his sport and profession continues to drive him on when he really has nothing more to prove. Kevin epitomises everything that is good about a coach. He is strong, committed, enthusiastic and with a huge, almost unquenchable, thirst for knowledge.

Kevin would explore the world and anything else available in his quest to better himself as a person and coach. That he has been so long at the one club, Essendon, is testament to his skills as a man, mentor and coach.

Tiko Jelisavcic, who coached the Socceroos for the 1965 World Cup qualifiers against North Korea, was instrumental in getting me to Australia. Tiko was a former Yugoslavian first division star who coached in the local league here before assuming the job with the national team.

He was a very smart man and was a professor of philosophy and I am glad to say I had a fabulous friendship with him. Tragically, he was killed in an accident while coaching in Mexico. His funeral was one of the biggest seen in Mexico with an estimated 60 000 attending the ceremony at the Azteca Stadium.

Who could forget 'Uncle' Joe Vlasits? He coached the

Socceroos from 1967 to 1970 as well as having a distinguished career in club football. Joe coached me when I had a guest stint with Yugal in Sydney in 1966.

Joe was a much loved and revered figure in Australian soccer because he was such an honest and kind-to-the-extreme person. I always thought it was a real disadvantage for him when it came to the players because they, more often than not, took advantage of his good-hearted nature.

Was he a good coach or not? I'll leave that for others. I will say, however, that he had a lot of good results. I eventually took over the Australian team from Joe in 1970.

Following my controversial sacking as Socceroos boss at the end of 1974, the game in this country went through a crazy period of about seven years in which the national team had a succession of coaches.

In my opinion, these guys were living proof of the disgraceful, disorganised and politically dirty workings of Australian soccer administration.

Green and Shoulder were Worthington's 'boys'—Englishman brought to this country under the national coaching scheme to allegedly enlighten us on how the game should be played. They were, unequivocally, disasters from the moment they stepped foot in the country.

The appointment of Green, who was coaching in the English fourth division at the time, and events subsequently turned our game into an absolute joke and it took years to recover from it. Green's career as Socceroos boss was a very short one.

As Lawrie Schwab reported, Green led the Australian team in a five-match series against the USSR in November 1975 before a match against Velez Mostar of Yugoslavia early in 1976. That was to be his last match. Not long after, he was caught and convicted of shoplifting and left Australia soon after, even though Arthur

George wanted him to stay on.

If Australian soccer thought its problems were over with Green's departure, it was badly mistaken!

Englishman Jimmy Shoulder's shock appointment rocked the game. He wasn't even in the picture, but got the job by default when Arthur's preferred option, Englishman Alan Vest, was dumped in a ballot after NSW turned on Arthur.

No sooner had Shoulder departed the scene than German Rudi Gutendorf arrived. He had some credentials, having coached the likes of Schalke, Duisburg and Hamburg in Germany, FC Lucerne in Switzerland and the Chilean national team.

He was a disaster from the moment he took over, turning over players like a butcher processes sausages. He introduced more players to the national team than any other coach in our history.

Gutendorf loved seeing his name in the media, whether it was for good or bad reasons, though I can't recall too many good times with him in charge of the national team. Eventually he was sacked in 1981 after Australia was dumped 2–0 by New Zealand at the Sydney Cricket Ground when our team was booed off the field after a disgraceful performance.

That was one of the saddest days of my life. It hurt me very much because I knew it should never have been that way. To this day, I believe, had I still be in charge of the Socceroos we would have again got to the World Cup.

But Arthur George, in all his stubbornness, could not see that. He had been hoodwinked by certain individuals for too long and was blind to what were his self-made disasters. He has a lot to answer for.

Once Gutendorf left, Les Scheinflug took over. Les was my assistant with the 1974 Socceroos. He was our first World Cup captain and scored our first goal in a World Cup qualifier. This man is an icon in our game and has done everything there is to achieve in Australian soccer.

While Les did much to help our game at senior level, he will always be remembered and revered for his remarkable contribution to youth soccer in this country. Over a 20-year period, he took the Young Socceroos (under 20s) and Joeys (under 17s) to amazing heights and helped produce some of our greatest talent.

Perhaps his greatest achievement was to take the Joeys to the final of the World Youth under 17s championship in New Zealand in 1999—the first time an Australian team had made the final of a World Cup. The Joeys were beaten in a penalty shoot-out by Brazil after the scores were locked 0–0 after extra time. I rate that as one of the greatest Australian sporting achievements of any code or level.

Sadly, Les only held the Socceroos job for two years before soccer politics and Arthur combined to get rid of him in favour of Frank Arok. When they sacked Les a part of him died, though, to his great credit, he continued to serve the game in a number of capacities over the years.

Frank and I grew up close together, but our paths never crossed until my teenage years, in the early 1950s. I knew of him because he was a staff coach at Novisad, then a second division club in Yugoslavia.

Frank was a very strong willed person, an intellectual and very dedicated. He was a journalist by occupation, but football was his life. He never played at the top level but it was incredible how much passion he had for the game.

I remember that even though he did not play at a top level, he would get up at 3am or 4am to practice his skills so he could show them off to the best players.

Frank came out to Australia in 1968 and took charge of the great St George club in NSW. I eventually took over from him at the club in August 1970, mainly on his recommendation to the

Saints board. Frank had decided to return home to Novisad.

We were always on good terms and I had a very high regard for his commitment. When I took over at St George I remember he left me with some incredible bookwork regarding coaching analysis, training regimes and schedules. It was very thorough and professional.

But things turned sour for some reason when he came back to Australia a second time. I had made a promise to Frank that St George, which had earned a reputation as a bridesmaid as far as winning trophies was concerned, that I would make the club a bride.

That was achieved when we won an international tournament in Tokyo in 1971 in what was possibly the greatest performance by an Australian club side. Later that year St George won the NSW grand final. I had kept my promise to turn the club into the bride. I left the club soon after and Frank came back to take over again at St George.

Frank was then strangely distant with me. Our relationship really soured in the early 1980s when he went on television and publicly criticised Les Scheinflug, who was then coach of the Socceroos.

I confronted him about it one day and could not help myself, 'You should be the father figure of coaching in this country, but what you did was unacceptable and unprofessional.'

As for his time as national coach, he did things way differently to what I would have done. The Socceroos had some good results, especially beating Yugoslavia 1–0 at the Seoul Olympics in 1988.

But for me, Frank lived on the night Australia beat an under-strength Argentina 4–1 at the Sydney Football Stadium in the Bicentennial Gold Cup in 1988. He became unbearable after that and I think it affected his judgment later on.

Frank eventually got the boot after two failed World Cup qualifying campaigns and I'll never forget the way he carried on after

Australia drew 1–1 with Israel at the SFS in 1989. The sight of Arok running on to the pitch and remonstrating like a mad-man with the referee because he considered the official had not added enough injury time was one of the most embarrassing and saddest sights I've seen.

Eddie Thomson took over from Arok in 1990 in an appointment that was well received by the media and fans in general. A likeable Scotsman, Eddie came to Australia in the late 1970s to link with Eastern Suburbs Hakoah as a player when the National Soccer League kicked off.

He assumed the coaching duties after a season and led the club, which had become known as Sydney City, to remarkable success. Eddie coached the same way he played—hard and tough and with a no-nonsense style.

Eddie was a great coach, very smart and tactically sound. He was a very direct person and said what he thought. He was such a fierce competitor and we had many ding-dongs when we opposed each other as club coaches.

Yes, we had some interesting times on the sidelines and there were often words passed between us. But there was always a mutual respect. We were professionals and we had a job to do.

I always liked Eddie's sense of humour. He was great at winding up people, having a lend of them. I remember I always enjoyed ringing him up on a Sunday morning before our teams played against each other.

One time I made a call and he answered with an abrupt, 'Who is speaking?'

I replied, 'Who else would ring you on the morning of a game?'

'Hello Rale, mate,' he said. I then asked him if he had a headache and he replied, 'Why?'

Quick as a flash I said, 'Because you have probably been up all night trying to work out how you are going to beat us and you know you don't have the answer!'

The reply was expected, 'Fuck off' as he slammed down the telephone.

That was Eddie for you, one of the real characters of the game—the type of people sadly missing from the sanitised version of the game these days.

There is no doubt in my mind that Eddie was extremely dedicated to the game and had a great football brain. But his greatest asset was his man-management. He was always on about togetherness and promoting a mateship environment. He was a player's coach and generally got the absolute best out of them.

As Socceroos boss, he had his share of wonderful results, none better than the 1–1 draw with the Maradona-led Argentina in a World Cup qualifier at the SFS in 1993. Maradona scored first after stealing the ball from Milan Ivanovic before Aurelio Vidmar equalised soon after. Sadly, the Socceroos lost the return leg in Argentina 1–0, thanks to a fluke of a goal.

Eddie should have taken the Socceroos to the 1997 World Cup qualifiers and he probably would have had he not been a victim of football politics. He was virtually forced to resign after then Soccer Australia chairman, David Hill, made life very difficult for him.

He resigned from his position in 1995 to take up a job in the J-League in Japan where he had quite reasonable success. He left a huge legacy for Australian Soccer because he was responsible for a golden era in the game by promoting the likes of Ned Zelic, Harry Kewell, Paul Okon and Milan Ivanovic to the national team.

One of the saddest days of my life was the day he passed away in 2003 after a courageous fight against cancer. My heart bled watching him waste away.

The highly credentialed Englishman, Terry Venables, eventually took over from Eddie after he went to Japan. Venables was a media magnet, one of the biggest names to come to this country.

He was a fantastic and gifted coach and his record speaks for itself. He earned the respect of the Socceroos even before they took the field for the first time under him. I guess he had that bit of Aussie larrikin in him and that's why he seemed to get on so well over here. I liked him because he was, as the English say 'a bit of a lad'. And there was no doubting he was a very good coach, who could get the best out of his players. He had played at a very high level, so he could talk on equal terms with the players, and they appreciated that.

Unfortunately, while he lost just two games during his stint with the Socceroos, he failed to deliver what he was paid huge money to do—get us to the 1998 World Cup finals in France.

Terry failed when it counted most and there isn't a soccer fan in the country who will ever forget the disaster at the MCG in 1997 when Australia, with the World Cup finals just 18 minutes away, threw away a two goal lead to eventually draw 2–2 with Iran and miss out on the away goals rule after the first game in Tehran had finished at 1–1.

I have never been involved in a more shattering night for our game. I was with most of the 1974 Socceroos after we had been paraded in open, luxury cars before the match. There was a huge sense of excitement and expectation as the game drew near. But I can tell you, it was a whole lot different when the final whistle went. Many of the 1974 Socceroos cried.

Poor Jimmy Mackay was totally devastated. He took the result very hard. Jimmy was sitting next to me when Iran scored their first goal. He could always read a game and how it was shaping. He turned to me and with tears in his eyes he said quietly, 'We are gone.' When Iran scored the second, the tears really flowed. He was stunned. He could not say a word.

Many people blame that serial pest, Peter Hoare, who ran on to the field and disrupted the game for five minutes when we were leading 2–0. But I blame Venables entirely for what happened that night.

Every coach dreams of being two goals up in a World Cup qualifier with time running out, but he failed to react to the situation of the pitch invader. Venables sat rooted to his seat on the sidelines. Nothing was done. No messages to the players, no hint of a substitute.

In my opinion, he should have ordered the players to close up the game and he should have brought on Milan Ivanovic to shore up the defence. Ivanovic was a wonderful player, one of the greatest football imports this country has had.

Venables made a terrible, terrible mistake by not starting the game with him and he compounded the error by not bringing him on when we led 2–0. If Terry still has a soft spot in his heart for Australia, if he still cares about the country then the name Milan Ivanovic will go over in his mind every day for the rest of his life.

Until Guus Hiddink's success in getting the Socceroos to the 2006 World Cup finals, Australia's flirtation with overseas coaches was a spectacular failure. It was alright to be taken in by the aura of overseas coaches, but the powers-that-be forgot that you had to have the right man. That man, Hiddink, finally came along in 2005.

It is interesting to note that before Hiddink's arrival, Australia's best results came when local coaches, or coaches who had learned their trade in this country, were in charge and not when the overseas coaches, the ones I called tourists, were in control.

Vlasits took the Socceroos to within a game of qualifying, we qualified under my reign, Arok fell at the final hurdle against Scotland in 1985 and Thomson also lost in the final match against Argentina in 1993, as did Frank Farina, who was in charge when the Socceroos needed only to draw in the second leg in

Montevideo in 2001 after winning the first leg 1–0 thanks to a Kevin Muscat penalty. They lost 3–0 in a result that devastated the game here.

And what of Farina? To be honest, I like the man. He has never done anything wrong by me. He is always polite and respectful whenever we speak. Unfortunately, he polarised people. You either liked him or hated him. There was no in between.

You won't get me saying too many nasty things about Frank's coaching though, I have to say I was shocked when he was given another four years as national coach after losing 3–0 to Uruguay. For me, he was too nice to be a coach and he could not separate being a coach from being one of the boys.

Anyway, how was that? Three Socceroos coaches who had failed in their first World Cup campaigns were all reappointed for a second bite—Arok, who saw out his second term, and Thomson and Farina, who both didn't get to complete their second chance. Yet, I was sacked after just four years and despite taking the Socceroos to the World Cup finals for the first time. Go figure!

Of course, Farina's reappointment had much to do with Soccer Australia's lack of finances at the time. The organisation was almost broke and could not afford big money for the national coach. I think Frank was on a pittance.

What a disgrace. The biggest job in the code had come down to dollars and cents. But it got worse for Farina.

I have never felt so embarrassed for our sport than when the FFA, which had taken control of the game after the SA board had been disbanded, ordered him to have anger management counselling after he clashed with an SBS journalist in the tunnel following an international against Iraq.

While the FFA was heavily criticised in some sections of the media for its decision, it was the beginning of the end for Frank. The wheels had been set in motion. When the Socceroos lost all three matches at the Confederations Cup—the prelude to the World Cup finals—in Germany in 2005, it was the straw that broke the camel's back as far as FFA chairman, Frank Lowy, was concerned.

Farina was the sacrificial lamb and Australian soccer was again plunged into controversy. Even the new guard was not immune from media criticism, thought it was all forgotten and forgiven when they unveiled Hiddink as the Socceroos saviour a month later.

Chapter 15
No Room for Kewell and Viduka

Talk about Australian footballers these days and two names automatically jump to mind—Harry Kewell and Mark Viduka. Yes, big names and big stars when it comes to public perception and media hype in this country.

And rightly so. Kewell (Liverpool, England) and Viduka (Middlesbrough, England) have been playing in top flight football in Europe for many years now and have built up reputations as outstanding players who would not be out of place on any football stage.

They are instantly recognisable around the world and their feats for their clubs have been extensively chronicled via television, radio and newspapers, both overseas and in Australia. Look at the Australian jerseys the kids wear these days and you can bet one or the other's name will be plastered on the back.

Not surprisingly, there are many followers here who regard them as among the greatest players produced in this country.

So it will come as a shock to many when I say that neither

would even make the bench in my greatest Socceroos side of all time. That's right—I can't find room for them in my top 17!

Nor, and it pains me to say it, is there a place in the starting XI for the late and much revered Johnny Warren, who has done more for the cause of Australian soccer than any 1000 administrators put together.

Unfortunately, John's cause as a player was not helped by a serious knee injury that would have ended the career of a lesser person. Such was his dedication, courage, will to win and hunger for success that he incredibly came back when he had been written off by almost everyone associated with the game.

There is no doubting Johnny's ability as a player. His game was based on his physical ability. He was so strong and commanding. He would go through brick walls and feel no pain. Sadly, Johnny was never quite the same player again after the injury and his strength and power was understandably missing from his game when he eventually made it back on to the field just before the World Cup finals.

Yes, I picked him in the 1974 Socceroos squad for West Germany and he played in the first match against East Germany. I saw that as a just reward for him, recognition for services given to Australian soccer. I wanted to show my respect for his determination and for his incredible fight back from a crippling injury. No one deserved it more.

As for Kewell and Viduka, don't get me wrong. I am full of admiration for what they have achieved over the years on the field and for what they have done for Australian football off it. They are phenomenal, extraordinarily talented players and deserve every reward that comes their way.

But as far as I am concerned, they have not really achieved anything in the game in regards to the Socceroos. In all seriousness, they have generally not produced when the Australian side had needed it most. A good case in point is the 1997 and 2001 World Cup qualifiers when the Socceroos depended so much on them for their experience and talent.

I know Viduka and Kewell, in particular, played strongly in the two qualifiers against Uruguay in 2005. Kewell was fabulous in the second game in Sydney and was one of the most influential players on the field at Telstra Stadium. Yet, for all of that, it isn't enough to sway my thinking. I can't help but hark back to the fact that both have not played for the Socceroos as often as I, and other fans, would have liked.

They have superstar status, but reputations mean nothing. It is success at all levels of the game that matters, not just club football.

For all his faults off the field, the controversial Mark Bosnich is a deep and realistic thinker when it comes to football and I will always remember an interview he did before the return leg World Cup qualifier against Iran in Melbourne in 1997.

When it was suggested to him by someone in the media that the then Terry Venables-coached Socceroos were the greatest Australian side of all time, Bosnich scoffed, 'The greatest side of all time is the 1974 Socceroos. They succeeded, we haven't.'

What Mark was saying was that the 1974 Socceroos were achievers. They went where no other Australian side had before—until the 2005 Socceroos.

And that's how I have based my all-time greatest Socceroos side. I have gone for special men who are passionate, who are achievers, fighters and the type who say 'follow me, I won't let you down'. Sure, maybe one or two would not be in the same class of a Kewell or Viduka, though that is a matter of opinion.

But I know whom I would want out there when the chips are down, the nation is on your shoulders and the world is looking at how you react.

In naming my best XI, I make no apologies for including eight players from the squad that played for the 1974 Socceroos—Doug Utjesenovic, Col Curran, Peter Wilson, Ray Richards, Jim Rooney, Jimmy Mackay, Ray Baartz and Adrian Alston.

It should be remembered that from the permanent Socceroos squad I had only one player—Manfred Schaefer—who never scored a goal. This highlighted the all round ability I was looking for in the squad.

The only three players outside of '74 are Bosnich, Milan Ivanovic and John Kosmina.

Of course, there will be people who don't know me—and never will—who will accuse me of living in the past. I am, supposedly, consumed by all things 1974. It's all I ever talk about. Nothing else matters.

Well that's total garbage, though I'll probably give them more ammunition to fire at me because of my selections! So, why I have chosen these players? Let's go through them one by one.

No 1. Goalkeeper—Mark Bosnich

For me, it came down to a choice between two players—Bosnich and former Adelaide City goalkeeper, Robert Zabica. I also rated Terry Greedy highly.

Zabica had the advantage of playing for so long under Zoran Matic, who instilled amazing discipline in all of his players. Robbie had a modest game, but was always solid and sound.

Bosnich was a freak, a real showman but, behind the extravagance, he was the complete package as a goalkeeper. He understood the game as well as any other player I have coached.

Mark exuded authority in his area and he was always in charge of his defence. Importantly, he was a big time player. I know his kicking wasn't a strong point, but I could suffer that because he was so brilliant in many other areas. If he had had Zabica's kicking game he would have been one of the greatest goalkeepers in the world.

No. 2. Right back—Doug Utjesenovic

There is no one to compare with Dougie. His European football education—he played among some of the best in Europe—made him a stand-out in Australia. Dougie had a superb temperament and I can't remember him ever receiving a yellow card.

He was an even better attacker than defender and scored some great goals and I have never seen a better crosser of a ball. Dougie also had a huge heart and showed it when he came back from a serious knee injury—the same that struck Johnny Warren—to play a number of years with St George in the old National Soccer League.

No. 3. Left back—Col Curran

Col was an aggressive, powerful and determined footballer and the kind that the strong soccer region of Newcastle is famous for producing. He wasn't a tall man, but he was extremely well built, with strong shoulders and a barrel chest. He had no fear and I am sure many of his opponents quivered in their boots at the mere sight of him.

Col was a brilliant overlapper and a much stronger tackler than Dougie, but they complemented each other. He also had a canon shot in both feet.

One of his greatest assets was his wonderful sense of humour and his contribution to the squad off the field. He was a real character and always terrific for team morale.

No. 4. Sweeper—Peter Wilson (captain)

Who else would you put in this position than this man-mountain of a character? Peter was a true leader, an inspiration, a man amongst men, a tower of strength. I get emotional every time I talk about him for I know what he was to Australian soccer and the 1974 Socceroos.

Football-wise, he was such an intelligent player in tactical terms. During a game he would only have to make eye contact with me and he knew instantly what I wanted.

Peter's stature—he was a strapping man with long, blond locks—was incredible. He just had a presence, an aura about him. A goliath amongst men. He was a strong, aggressive player, simplistic to the extreme. He was always the same whether at training or in a game. He gave 100 per cent.

Peter Wilson was, in my mind, our greatest captain ever.

No. 5. Stopper—Milan Ivanovic

Here was a complete footballer. Milan had a tremendous background. He played with distinction in Yugoslavia with Red Star and was simply outstanding when he came to Australia to play under Zoran Matic at Adelaide City.

It was always a case of when, not if, he would play for the Socceroos and Eddie Thomson deserves a vote of gratitude for having the foresight to pick him. Milan had a magic touch and an incredible temperament on the field. Off the field you could not hope to meet a nicer person. He was a thorough gentleman and I have never heard a bad word said against him by player, official or media.

What I liked most about Milan was his ability to transfer defence into attack with just two touches. His technique was better than many attacking players.

No. 6. Midfield—Ray Richards

I have him in my side for a specific reason. Every team must have a very disciplined, tactically mature player who can act as a defender and attacker equally well. He was that type of player. He was my key to the midfield.

Ray was built like Curran, shortish, but with very broad shoulders and barrel-chested. He was so tough and strong and another player who had no fear.

Ray, who was also a real character, was renowned for his long throw-ins...my goodness, he could throw a ball longer than some players could kick it! That was a huge advantage because he could throw the ball into the opposition penalty area from almost any part of the field.

Who could forget his greatest moment when he marked the great Pele in a Socceroos v Santos match at the old Sydney Football Stadium? Ray was phenomenal that day and Pele, the greatest player in the world, could hardly get a kick.

Ray was once a striker, which explains why he had a powerful shot in both feet. He could score goals from 20 to 30 metres. He was deadly.

No. 7. Midfield—Jimmy Rooney

A stocky Scotsman, Jimmy wasn't overly big, but he had powerful legs and unbelievable strength.

He was a human dynamo. He was so powerful and had tremendous close skills and was another with a super temperament and wonderful personality. His greatest asset was that he was very cunning and could generally out-think his opponents. He was always a step or two ahead.

Jimmy was honest to extremes and could run all day. He formed a super partnership on and off the field with Jimmy Mackay and Richards. He was one of the most loyal people I have ever met.

No. 8. Midfield—Jimmy Mackay

Another Scotsman, he was only slightly bigger than his great mate Jimmy Rooney.

He will always be remembered for scoring THE goal that got us to the World Cup finals, but there was much, much more to Jimmy. He was an incredible marker and a remarkable ball winner. He could steal the ball off you before you realised what had happened. I lost count of the number of non-plussed looks on the faces of his rivals after he had stolen the ball from them.

He was one of the most simplistic players ever and had a knack of transferring defence into attack with one ball and following up to finish off with a shot on goal.

Amazingly, Jimmy always hated training but you could always bet he would bring his best game to a match, especially the big occasions.

No. 9. Striker—Ray Baartz

What can I say about him? Probably the best way to sum up Ray is to declare that, in my opinion, he is the greatest player Australia has produced. Throw them all in—Kewell, Viduka, Reg Date, Joe Marston. None of them match up to him.

In fact, give Ray every number from one to 11 for he was the Socceroos and even his team-mates thought he was the team.

Ray had everything as a player from skill, to fantastic temperament to an explosive shot with both feet, to powerful heading. He played the most remarkable one touch football. I have never seen a more complete player.

If Ray had a fault it was that he was too quiet at times, though it never detracted from his beautiful sense of humour. The big thing about him is that he never had an enemy in his life.

I have no doubts that had Ray not been cut down by that vicious karate chop to the neck against Uruguay before the 1974 World Cup finals, we would have fared much, much better than walking away with a single point.

No. 10. Striker—Adrian Alston

This was possibly the hardest choice to make for me involving two fantastic players in Adrian and Atti Abonyi.

Atti was such a gifted player. He could do anything on the field, but he had a fault in that he was generally a better player at home than away while Adrian was fantastic in just about any situation.

I went for Adrian because he was a stronger player in a tight situation. He was a match winner. He was very fast, very mobile and had incredible heading ability and, importantly, was a big match player. It was always said that when he was 'on', the team was 'on'. Noddy was good enough to play in England (Luton Town and Cardiff City) and also found his way to America where he played with the superbly gifted Englishman Rodney Marsh at the Tampa Bay Rowdies. You can only imagine what these two extroverts got up to?

Adrian was also some character. He has a heart of gold and works with disabled people in Wollongong. He is a great story-teller and mesmerises you with his tales. He could sing, too, and that really made him the life of the party and fantastic for team spirit.

No. 11. Striker—John Kosmina

This was another tough choice between Kosmina and Branko Buljevic. Branko was a bit of a maligned player and never got the credit he deserved.

John gets the nod because he was a deadly striker. I don't think we have seen too many better finishers in this country than him.

Kosmina had a fabulous competitive attitude. He hated losing—a trait built into him during his days with the all-conquering Sydney City in the National Soccer League. He was strong and extremely aggressive and it is something he has carried off the field. John is never afraid to speak his mind. Just like his playing days, he never takes a step backwards. He is your typical Aussie bastard. He fears no-one.

As a long-time Socceroos captain, he led by example though I believe that, as a player, he never realised his full potential. I remember when he tried his luck with Arsenal in England. Unfortunately, he never coped with the conditions, which is a shame. Had he stuck at it he could have been anything.

These days John is making a name for himself as a coach in the new A-League with Adelaide United. He led Adelaide to the minor premiership in the first season of the league, showcasing the wonderful local coaching talent we have in this country.

As for my bench, it would be made up of: John Warren, John Watkiss, Robbie Zabica, Atti Abonyi, Zarko Odzakov and Alan Davidson.

Chapter 16

More Club Success and Life Outside of Football

After returning from the World Cup I guess it took a few years to realise I wouldn't get the chance to coach the Socceroos again, certainly not with Arthur George still having a vice-like grip on control of the Australian Soccer Federation.

The fans, the run-of-the-mill football administrators and the media gave me great support, but my differences with Arthur were irreconcilable. As long as he was still in charge I was 1000-1 to be recalled to take over the national job. Given he kept his position of extreme power until 1988—14 years after we had qualified for the World Cup finals—there was never any coming back for me.

Despite that, I threw myself in to the sport that has been my passion and my life. I coached Pan Hellenic for two years (1974–75) and we had a good run in the NSW first division, though it had its moments, as it always does at this volatile and passionate club.

There was a day at Hurstville Oval when we led 1–0 and were looking good against the Joe Vlasits coached St George, until the

Saints let loose. They replied with six straight goals and the Greek fans were not happy! The fans had a reputation for venting their disgust in an intimidating fashion—rude hand gestures, verbal abuse, throwing rubbish and milling around the ground after a match to voice their displeasure.

You didn't need to be a genius to work out I was going to cop it and, to their credit, the police also sensed there would be trouble. As I was walking off the field with the fans getting more agitated by the minute, the sergeant in charge came up to me and said, 'We are here for you, no need to worry.'

I told him politely not to worry about me because I knew how to handle the situation. 'There's no need, sir,' I said. 'I know these people and I know how to handle them.' He was rather taken aback and insisted, 'But Mr Rasic, we have to protect you. This could get very nasty.'

I held my ground. 'Look, you can stay close but stay reasonably well behind me,' I said. 'That's unthinkable,' the sergeant said. 'We have to do our job. It is our responsibility to ensure this does not get out of hand and no-one is seriously hurt.' Again, I insisted. 'I promise you, they will not move. They will not lay a finger on me.' He reluctantly relented.

Later, as I emerged from the dressing room I was greeted by a huge group of fans. 'What about that, Mr Rasic?' one fan screamed out. I turned to him and apologised for the loss. 'I promise you, it won't happen again,' I said. With that, the situation was diffused. The sergeant was amazed. I told him, 'You have to know these people. You have to know their passion for the club. If you treat them properly and with respect they will give you no trouble. If you stir them, infuriate them or treat them like idiots then you are asking for trouble.'

In the second season, we reached the preliminary final, but lost to Apia in the 119th minute. While I did not get them the championship they so wanted, I loved the club and I loved the people in the stands and in the street who followed it. I didn't like the petty politics and back-stabbers.

In my time at the club, I helped produce players like Gary Meier, Richie Bell and Chris Thamnidis, who all went on to serve the club admirably. Then there was Gary Manuel, Dave Harding and Ivo Rudic who all became '74 Socceroos.

Pan Hellenic, later to be known as Sydney Olympic, should have been the biggest club in Australian soccer. It had a huge base of fans but the people who ran the club generally failed it. Look, you couldn't fault their passion but they lacked vision and foresight.

The club never really had a home ground or proper training facilities. It roamed from area to area and ground to ground. They tried to get licensed clubs up and running, like Marconi, but it just didn't work. Sadly, Olympic play in the NSW super league these days. They just didn't have the money to be part of the A-League.

From Pan Hellenic I went to Marconi for what was to be its last season in the NSW competition. In 1975 a number of clubs in NSW, Victoria, South Australia and Queensland, under the guidance of Frank Lowy (Hakoah)—yes, that Frank Lowy, now chairman of Football Federation Australia—and Alex Pongrass (St George), got together and agreed to form what was to be the most exciting initiative seen in Australian soccer—the National Soccer League.

This was a huge breakthrough for the game. It would unite the states and clubs and provide top class competition, which would help produce wonderful players, great entertainment and more media coverage.

Fourteen teams—five from NSW, four from Victoria, two from Brisbane and South Australia and one from Canberra—kicked off the first season amid much fanfare in 1977. Marconi was one of those clubs and we boasted a great squad that included Alan

Maher, Jimmy Rooney, Ray Richards, Ernie Campbell, Paul Degney, Gary Byrne, Ivo Prskalo, Peter Sharne and Bertie Mariani.

We opened up a big break at one stage and looked like romping away with the championship, but things started to go wrong for us late in the season. In fact, we fell into a big hole.

This allowed Sydney City to catch up. The championship, which was decided by the first first-past-the-post system, went down to the last match of the season. In the end, Sydney City pipped us on goal difference for the inaugural title. It was a terrible blow, but the season wasn't a waste. I was voted coach-of-the-year and Rooney was voted player-of-the-year. In that season, a budding young star was named under 21 player-of-the-year—John Kosmina.

Marconi finished fourth in 1978, the season the great Italian international Roberto Vieri, the father of super goalscorer, Christian, who has played for some of the biggest clubs in the world and is an Italian international himself, played with us and thrilled the fans with his supreme skills.

Roberto was an extraordinary player. He had a glittering career playing in the Italian Seria A and played many times for the Italian national team. While he was at the wrong end of his career when he came here, he was nonetheless a revelation for Australian soccer fans.

He had a mop of grey hair and looked like he would be lucky to last 10 minutes, let alone 90 minutes in the NSL. But looks are deceiving. Roberto was the master and the rest were his pupils. He controlled nearly everything on the field with his unbelievable vision, skill and precise passing. And he could score a goal, too, especially from free-kicks which he would bend around a defensive wall like a banana.

The next year I joined Adelaide City—a big, big club which regularly drew crowds of more than 12 000. We finished fifth in the two seasons I was there which was a huge disappointment given I had some great players in John and Bugsy Nyskohus, Gary Marocchi, John Perin, Agenor Muniz and the unbelievable Dixie Deans. However, we won the NSL Cup beating St. George 3–2 in the final in 1979.

I will always have fond memories of Deans, one of the greatest characters and footballers, I have ever dealt with. He was a legend when he played with Scottish giants Celtic in the 1970s and he ended up playing about four seasons—on and off—in Adelaide.

What a player. He was incredibly strong and quick and could score goals from anywhere. He ended up scoring 30 goals in 53 matches for City and the fans absolutely idolised him. Sometimes in your career as a coach you are just privileged to be involved with some players, and that's how I felt about Dixie and Vieri.

They were class acts. Roberto wasn't as good a trainer as Dixie. In fact, Roberto was a shocker. He couldn't run, he wouldn't run. He was always saving himself up for a game. With Roberto and Dixie, you always knew they would turn up for a game and be at their best.

I remember a game against Sydney City, whicn had the likes of Steve O'Connor, Murray Barnes, Ernie Campbell, Todd Clarke, Hilton Silva, the late Eddie Thomson and Joe Watson and the tough man of the league, Kevin Mullen, at Wentworth Park in 1979. We were down 2–0 and in all sorts of trouble until Dixie took matters into his own hands.

He started verbally tormenting Mullen, a brave move considering Mullen had a huge reputation for toughness. Mullen was a lovely man and a great footballer but he was also a maniac on the field and would easily lose his cool.

'Let me get the ball and I'll fucking put it through your legs every time,' Dixie kept saying to Mullen. Eventually, it happened. But not only did Dixie put the ball through his legs, but he then went past Thommo and O'Connor to score and make it 2–1.

Dixie started to take the piss out of Mullen. 'You are going to fucking get subbed after that,' he said to him. Not long after Dixie got past Mullen again and scored to make it 2–2. As Mullen was walking off after being subbed, Dixie said, 'Leaving us so soon?' But Dixie wasn't finished. He scored another goal to give him a hat-trick and we won 3–2.

Even though Dixie was a fearless player, he had one weakness…spiders. He was terrified by them and the players never missed the chance to tell him about redbacks and funnelwebs and how they have been known to kill people.

One day the joker of the squad, Agenor Muniz, set him up brilliantly. Agie got hold of a fake spider and spring. He placed it in an envelope, wrapped it up, put some Hong Kong stamps on it and addressed it to 'The great Scottish legend Dixie Deans.'

The wrapped box was handed to Dixie at a team meeting and he turned to me proudly and said, 'See boss, fans all around the world love me.' When Dixie opened the box, the fake spider popped out and struck him. You have never seen a grown man react with such fear. He screamed out 'my God!' and jumped out of his chair so far he almost hit the ceiling. It took the players hours to stop laughing.

It was during my first season in Adelaide that, along with some businessmen, I arranged for the New York Cosmos to come to Australia. The Cosmos played in the North American League and included some of the biggest names in world football such as Franz Beckenbauer, Giorgio Chinaglia, Carlos Alberto, Vladomir Bogicevic and Johan Neeskens, who is now an assistant coach with the Socceroos.

Cosmos lost to Australia, coached by Rudi Gutendorf, 2–1 at the Sydney Showground when more than 70 000 fans turned up, catching officials by surprise. It was a huge success and the ground authorities had to let a large number of fans in for free because of safety fears outside.

Cosmos also beat Adelaide City 2–0 in front of 22 000 fans in Adelaide.

Blacktown City Demons were an ambitious club and I joined them after leaving Adelaide at the end of the 1980 season. It was a disaster. The Demons were too small a club for too big a step. We finished second last and were relegated.

I had 1982 off before joining Victorian giants, South Melbourne, who were craving success. Despite having great players, money and passion they just couldn't win a championship or cup. I describe my season there as a tragedy for the club which simply imploded through internal politics.

South Melbourne finished fourth, just three points from champions St George. At least I had the satisfaction of bringing some great players to the club like Oscar Crino, Kenny Murphy, Bobby Russell and Doug Brown and that created a base for South Melbourne to win two NSL championships.

I had two seasons off this time before I was lured to the Italian-backed Apia Leichhardt, one of the most famous clubs in NSW football. I spent the next three years there.

In 1987 Apia created the record for going most games unbeaten—23—before winning the championship by six points from Preston. The season was one of the greatest I've been involved in. We had a fantastic squad with the likes of Socceroos captain Charlie Yankos, Arno Bertogna, Jean-Paul de Marigny, Peter Katholos, Rod Brown, Tony Pezzano, Terry Greedy, Peter Tredinnick, Alex Bundalo, Burim Zajmi, Mark Brown, Gary Ward and Terry Butler.

A group of a prominent Italian businessman was a huge factor for us, helping to provide us with everything we needed.

More honours came the club's way when I was named NSL coach-of-the-year for the second time in my career. Only Eddie Thomson (3), Frank Arok, Bertie Mariani and Mirko Bazic (2) had won it twice or more. Apia also won the national cup in 1988, beating Brunswick Juventus.

The biggest thrill in terms of awards that came my way was in 1989 when I was inducted in to the Australian Sporting Hall of Fame and my name now sits along side some of the greatest sports men and women this country has seen. To be included among the likes of Sir Donald Bradman, Dawn Fraser, Rod Laver, Ron Clarke, Ron Barassi, John Betrand, Ken Rosewall, John Konrads and Murray Rose is something that is beyond belief for me. Nothing can be compared with it.

After a four-year break I had a two-season stint at Parramatta Eagles (1992–93, 1993–94), taking the club to the play-offs for the first time in its NSL history. We also lost the Cup final to Heidelberg United, coached by the great Dragoslav Sekularac, with the last kick of the ball.

Parramatta was a good club but, once again, officialdom got in the way and ruined things. Some people simply got too big for their boots. The second season did not go so well and we finished eight points out of the play-offs but we won the national cup 2–0, beating Sydney United, which included the likes of current Socceroos Tony Popovic and Zeljko Kalac as well as Ante Milicic, Mark Babic and Manis Lamond.

Still, I was happy with the job I had done at the club with some great young talent emerging such as Gabriel 'Chi Chi' Mendez, Brendan Renaud, Joe Spiteri, Michael Reda, Glenn Gwynne and Paul Souris while that magician Marshall Soper and the late Geoff Gunning were inspirational.

After leaving Parramatta I thought that was the end of coaching. To be honest, I had had enough. I was looking in different directions now.

As I recounted in an earlier chapter regarding my days in the orphanage when we used to get involved in making soccer balls out of pigs bladders, then covering them in the yarn, I have always enjoyed creating things, coming up with ideas—and organising who does what.

As a coach I came up with the ideas, but I used someone else's feet to get the job done. In later years, however, I was fortunate enough to come up with certain ideas, call them inventions, that created opportunities for players, young and old, to overcome obstacles on the training field or in their backyards.

I found that in Australia kids and senior players, many of whom had superb physical qualities, lacked technique, co-ordination, balance and timing in vital areas that would make a huge difference to their success or otherwise.

A good case in point is in heading a ball, which is one of the most important, yet difficult aspects of the game. Some great players are able to hang up in the air for what seems seconds. They make it look so easy. German Uwe Seeler was unbelievable in this regard. Another German, Gerd Muller, wasn't very tall at all but scored some magnificent goals with his head.

In Australia, Max Tolson and Adrian Alston were two of the greatest exponents of heading a ball I have seen. Tolson, who had great technique, was always brilliant in timing his leap and that is where his strength came from. Alston was nicknamed Noddy because he was so good in the air.

I introduced a fixed apparatus at Blacktown City in 1981 which supported a suspended ball, but it wasn't quite what I wanted. I forgot about the idea until about 1991 when I decided I would invent a portable apparatus. I wanted something that could be easily assembled and disassembled, was portable and could fit into any sized car.

I lost count of the number of people here who came up with plenty of reasons why it couldn't be done. But I wasn't one to be put off at all. Armed with a large plastic container with my bits and pieces, I went to the United States in 1993. I went to Texas, where I had an academy of soccer, and was introduced to Kevin Currey, a quadriplegic who, before his unfortunate car accident, had a huge engineering business which went bankrupt because of his problems.

I consulted with him about my idea and he liked it immediately. Despite his huge disability, Kevin managed to master a computer and showed me so many ideas and short cuts. He was also brilliant in regards to organising patents because he knew all the rules and had so many contacts.

It took three months to perfect the apparatus, then came the interesting part. Normally it can take up to five years for a patent to be approved in the United States, but through Kevin we got it in 17 months. It was so good that I got a letter from the Department of Patents, congratulating me and awarding a certificate for originality, simplicity and innovation. It has also been officially endorsed by FIFA, the sport's governing body. I was now a bona fide inventor, no Thomas Edison or Marconi, but an inventor just the same!

That really gave me a good kick. I developed other training aides, one of which was endorsed by Soccer NSW, which is now one of my biggest customers. Before that, however, I had gone to the AIS in the mid 1990s with all my inventions, seeking an endorsement from them. I was referred from one department to another and, in the end, I was given a 'thanks but no thanks'.

So much for being one of the original five-person panel—myself, Dr Allan Coles (director of and professor for the school of physical education), the late Jack Clarke (former Essendon VFL captain), Andrew Dettre (journalist and secretary to the minister Tourism and Recreation), Dr Ken Fitch (Australian Olympic team physician in 1972) and Elaine Murphy (lecturer in recreation)—that laid the foundation for the development of the AIS.

Still, once a coach, always a coach. I made one of the biggest mistakes of my football career when I was talked into taking over at Canberra near the end of the 1997–1998 season. I also took them into the following season. And that is about as much as I want to say about that part of my career. In describing my time at Canberra I would prefer to leave one, big blank page in this book, under the heading Canberra. The best thing about Canberra was the highway back to Sydney.

After all the problems I had with Australian soccer officialdom, I was inducted into Soccer Australia's Roll of Honour in 1999. It was a fantastic gesture but, still, they could not get it totally right. The framed award was given to me and a copy is supposed to be hanging up in the office of the FFA along with a lot of the other inductees over the years. But would you believe that my award is the only one missing from the FFA's wall of fame? I have asked many times where has the award gone and no-one seems to know the answer. Am I still paying for my supposed sins of 1974?

The year 2000 provided me with another highlight when I was awarded the Australian Sports Medal by the Queen and, in 2001, I was awarded a Centennial Medal. In 2002 I was awarded an Order of Australia.

After the debacle at Canberra, it was another three years before I would be involved in NSL club level again. Having sworn never to coach again, I was lured by a good offer to take over as Football Manager at Marconi for the 2002–2003 season.

Now this was the greatest mistake I've ever made, without question.

Given my past success with the club, my huge love for it, the people, the atmosphere and the fact I was a life-member, this should have been my dream job. What more could I have asked?

But times had changed and so had the thinking of the people who were now running the club. They were clueless and I don't think too many of them had the Marconi Stallions or soccer at heart. You only have to look now at what has happened to this once great and admired football club.

Marconi is playing in the NSW super league, having let its fans and the district of Fairfield-Liverpool down by electing not to try and get a franchise in the new A-League. In my opinion, they have abandoned the superbly talented youth of the south western suburbs of Sydney.

I should have guessed the club had lost its passion for the game by the way they treated me in my last stint there. Instead of concentrating on helping (coach) Raul Blanco run the football, I was forever at finance meetings trying to justify the soccer section's budget. I tell you, I felt more like federal government treasurer, Peter Costello, than a football manager after those meetings with the Marconi licensed club board.

In the end, I was forced to take over coaching the side for the last 10 games of the season after I was made to sack Raul, saving the Stallions from being handed the wooden spoon for the first time in their history. We needed to win our last game of the season at home against subsequent champions Perth Glory to do it. We won 2–0.

I expected something drastic would happen once the season was over, and it did. My contract expired and there was no way the club was going to renew it. It wasn't the first time it had happened to me and I would normally have accepted it and just walked away.

But what happened after that marked me forever. After being delivered a letter telling me to vacate the office by 5pm that day, I was escorted out of the club by an official. He was a nice man and it wasn't his fault, but I could not believe it was happening to me and at the club that had been a huge part of me.

I have never felt so embarrassed, so humiliated. The official looked at me and said, 'Let's just keep walking.' After that I vowed never to step foot inside the club again.

But I broke that vow and with good reason, in November 2004. I was asked to attend the final of the Johnny Warren Cup at Marconi Stadium between John's and my old club, St George, and Bonnyrigg White Eagles after John had passed away a week earlier following his long fight with cancer.

I haven't been inside the club since and I won't ever be back. Marconi is just not the same any more.

Chapter 17

My Ten Greatest Games

As a coach you look back on your career and the games you have been involved in. There are 10 matches which will always remain in my heart for various reasons. I'll start from the bottom and work my way up.

No. 10: Australia 2 v Uruguay 0
Sydney Cricket Ground, April 27 1974

This was so specific for confidence and so important for me, especially after that clash with Arthur George several days earlier following the 0–0 draw with Uruguay at Olympic Park in Melbourne.

It was also a sad occasion after losing Ray Baartz with that shocking injury. Our confidence was so high after drawing in Melbourne and it was important to keep things on a high. I knew Uruguay would be much tougher and much smarter in this game and I told the players so.

Uruguay's national pride would not allow it to contemplate losing to us or even drawing. Whenever Uruguay played, it wasn't a friendly. Its national pride wouldn't allow it. The South Americans played for their land.

Unfortunately for Uruguay, the Socceroos were capable of beating even better teams than it…such was our supreme dominance at the SCG that day. The media went absolutely crazy over that result, though they paid more attention to Ray's injury.

In a way, they probably helped us because it took the focus away from the team and how well we had played. It kept us out of the limelight and out of the minds of our World Cup opponents.

No. 9: Australia 3 v Greece 1
Athens, 1970

And the world takes notice.

This result during the first world tour, made headlines all over Europe. It was a real feather in our caps to beat the Greeks in front of their own people.

I received so many calls from journalists and coaches all over Europe, especially the British media. The result was a huge boost and gave all of us great confidence. Remember, it was Greece's first defeat in three years on home soil.

Helmet Shoen, the West German manager, was so impressed he rang assistant coach Les Scheinflug to find out how we had beaten Greece. They played them three days later and also won 3–1 in Athens.

That game also marked my first clash with then captain John Warren.

No. 8: Australia 0 v West Germany 3
Hamburg, June 18 1974

Our second appearance in the World Cup finals against one of the biggest footballing nations in the world. The Germans had won the European Championship in 1972 and were among the favourites to win the World Cup final with Italy, Brazil, Holland and East Germany.

Franz Beckenbauer, Gerd Muller, Sepp Maier, Paul Breitner, Wolfgang Overath, Berti Voigts and Uli Hoeness. What a team! The great Gunter Netzer could not even make the side.

The West Germans had 70 000 fans behind them and they were baying for blood. The expectation was that we would cop six, seven, even eight goals. It didn't happen.

In the end, the fans were booing their own team and cheering for us in the second half.

No. 7: Australia 0 v Chile 0
Berlin, June 22 1974

Our first point in the finals.

Chile was the second-best side in South America after finishing behind Brazil in their qualifiers. The Chileans had drawn 0–0 with East Germany and lost 1–0 to West Germany to a Brietner free-kick before meeting us in the final game of the preliminary round at the World Cup.

The match was played in dreadful conditions with constant rain falling for most of the match. Both teams had great character.

Our desire was not to leave the tournament without at least a point. We were determined not to lose to the Chileans. We were under all sorts of pressure before the rain came, but turned it back on them in the wet conditions.

No. 6: Australia 0 v East Germany 2
Hamburg, June 14 1974

Our build up for our first appearance at the World Cup finals was phenomenal. No detail was spared. A lot of work went into this game.

Our lead-up games against Indonesia, Israel and three matches in Switzerland was all geared for the tournament, but this match in particular. We had the eyes of the world on us and we wanted to make a good impression. We did not want to disgrace ourselves.

The biggest compliment was that the East Germans had spies watching us train and play in Switzerland.

We performed beyond expectations against the robots of European football. We lost 2–0 but it was a super performance and captured the hearts of the home fans and world media.

Sadly, we missed Ray Baartz in this match. Had we had him, we could well have produced one of the greatest upsets in world football.

No. 5: Australia 3 v Iraq 1
Sydney, March 1973

So much technical detail went into this game. It was not just about the players, but what happened behind the scenes.

The input of a wide range of people, including Lou Brocic and the groundsmen played a huge part. We had every piece of information possible about our opponents, thanks to Lou. He also pointed out that the Iraqis never wear screw in studs.

This is where the groundsmen played an important role. The Iraqis were slipping and sliding on the old Sports Ground surface.

In this match Adrian Alston was on fire and midfielders Ray Richards and Jimmy Mackay lived up to their big match reputations. That we scored three goals was a huge bonus for goal difference was to playa huge role for us.

I was furious when we conceded a goal in the 90th minute.

No. 4: Australia 3 v Iran 0
Sydney, July 1973

How important scoring three goals in this match was evident in the return leg in Tehran a week later.

This was the most complete performance of any Australian team at a ground—the Sydney Sports Ground—that became our home.

Atti Abonyi's second goal, from the kick-off, was something you don't see too often. It was a master goal as the Iranians did not touch the ball before it went in. Atti was a special player when he was at his best.

The team was on its game from the start. The defence, marshalled by Peter Wilson and including Col Curran, Doug Utjesenovic and John Watkiss, was as solid as a rock.

No. 3: Australia 2 v South Korea 2 Seoul, November 10 1973

This is a game when some people thought we were dead and buried and that our World Cup dream was gone. How wrong!

The dramas started when we arrived in Seoul and were kept inside customs for two and a half hours. All through the lead-up the Koreans were trying to play tricks on us, but they were dealing with a remarkable group of men who were not prepared to bow.

After just 29 minutes we were 2–0 down and no-one thought we could fight back, including team manager John Barclay. But nothing could stop this team. They had enormous desire and a will to win unmatched by most nations. We scored just before half time and equalised just after the break and should have gone on to win but for hitting the woodwork several times.

No. 2: Australia 0 v Iran 2 Tehran, August 24 1973

Even in defeat, we were winners. This could be rated as one of the greatest human efforts by an Australian national sporting team.

With 100 000 fans baying for our blood and spurring their team on we were under tremendous pressure—the sort of pressure that would have crushed a team of lesser men.

The Iranians needed to win 3–0 to force extra time or 4–0 to qualify for the World Cup finals, and they gave it their best shot.

They led 2–0 after 15 minutes and were headed for glory.

But they did not count on our huge spirit. Jimmy Fraser, Wilson, Utjesenovic, Watkiss, Curran and Richards were phenomenal. In fact, they were all outstanding.

But it was Max Tolson who turned it all around by inspiring the team at half time, first with some incredible words, then through his deeds on the field. He terrorised the Iranians.

One thing should be said, the Iranian officials and media were superbly respectful, dignified and polite in defeat. I think they knew the Socceroos were something special and there was glory in defeat for them.

No. 1: Australia 1 v South Korea 0
Hong Kong, November 13 1973

There cannot be another game to match this. It has gone down in Australian sporting folklore. And remained that way for another 32 years.

Confidence was sky high after the remarkable comeback from two goals down in Seoul. There was no way we were going to lose this game.

How many times has Jimmy Mackay's thunderball goal from way outside the box in the 75th minute been replayed not only in Australia, but all over the world?

From the 75th minute until the 90th minute—it was without doubt the longest 15 minutes of my life.

Our arrival in Sydney after that victory was one of the greatest moments of my career and will stay with me for the rest of my life.

Chapter 18
Why?

When Australian striker John Aloisi kept his nerve, sent the ball in to the left hand corner of the net and set off on his jubilant run around Telstra Stadium on that wonderful November night in 2005 after the penalty shoot-out win over Uruguay in the second leg World Cup qualifier, a tidal wave of relief, joy and emotion swept the nation.

At last, after 32 years of heartbreak, near misses and recriminations, the Socceroos were going to the World Cup again. It was a moment many thought they would never get to see.

Having not been invited as a special guest by Football Federation Australia, instead taking up a guest-speaking engagement at a function before the game, I was privileged to be part of the night and the amazing atmosphere, an atmosphere I have never seen the like of in Australia at any sporting event except, maybe, for the night Cathy Freeman won the 400m gold at the Sydney Olympics in 2000.

This was a nation united and for once the football gods decided to smile upon the Socceroos. It was not before time.

This time everything seemed to be going our way. Uruguay

missed a couple of gift chances and there were no freaks running on to the ground to disrupt the match *a la* serial pest Peter Hoare, who raced on to the field when the Socceroos were leading 2–0 against Iran at the MCG in 1997 and tore down one of the nets. Some say that incident cost the Socceroos the game, though I don't really subscribe to that theory.

But the biggest and most important factor we had going for us was on the sidelines in the form of Dutch master coach Guus Hiddink, who had waltzed into Australian soccer like a breath of fresh air just four months earlier to replace Frank Farina, who had been sacked as national coach.

What an inspired appointment by FFA chairman, Frank Lowy. Lowy, the head of Westfield, knew who he wanted to replace Farina. He went after his man and, as you would expect from Lowy, he got him.

Australia had signalled it meant serious business by luring a man with an incredible coaching pedigree. Hiddink had taken Holland and South Korea to the World Cup finals and has a list of accomplishments in club coaching in Europe the length of your arm.

Still, there were the doubters who suggested that four months was not enough for him to get to know the Socceroos players and to change things around. You needed at least two years, possibly more they claimed.

It had taken me four years to build, blend then refine the 1974 Australians for our assault on the World Cup. But they were different times. The game has moved on dramatically since then. In my mind, Hiddink's appointment was a master stroke and I firmly believed he could do the job.

After all, he is a very smart, educated man. He knows his way around world football and he didn't take the Socceroos job without careful consideration nor did he go in to it thinking there was no chance for success. That he turned a team in disarray, a team that leaked goals like a sieve, a team given no chance of qualifying for the World Cup just four months earlier, in to a world class side in such a short space of time is testament to his marvellous coaching skills.

Of course, sometimes you need luck and it has often been said that one can make one's own luck. Guus showed his human side as a coach and had luck on his side during in the second leg against Uruguay. With five minutes of extra time to go, he was warming up substitute goalkeeper Zeljko Kalac, getting him ready to replace Mark Schwarzer for the penalty shoot-out because he considered Kalac better in those situations.

He obviously did not know that Mark is a fantastic keeper in shoot-outs as he showed when he became a sporting hero after rescuing the Socceroos in the World Cup qualifier against Canada at Aussie Stadium in 1993. As fate would have it, Brett Emerton was injured soon after and Guus had to use his last replacement on the field. Kalac sat back on the bench.

Schwarzer made two outstanding saves in the penalty shoot-out to earn him a special place in Australian soccer history and in the hearts of the millions of fans around the country.

Now that Dutchman Hiddink has got the Socceroos to the World Cup who knows what else he has in store or how far the Australian team can go. Look what he did with South Korea four years ago. The Koreans were the Cinderella story of the 2002 World Cup finals, coming from nowhere to reach the semi-finals in one of the great achievements in world soccer history.

Certainly the Socceroos are on course to score our first goal in the World Cup finals and are capable of grabbing our first win. Yes, they have drawn a tough group with championship favourites Brazil, Croatia and Asian giants, Japan.

But don't underestimate them, especially with Hiddink in

charge. A second round berth is not beyond them.

If we had had a coach the calibre of Hiddink years ago, I have absolutely no doubt that while we would not have qualified for every World Cup, we would have qualified at least three times in the last 32 years.

Now we are on the big stage, Australian soccer's great march should not stop here. The Socceroos admission into the Asian confederation this year means a much fairer World Cup qualifying path than in the past and we should be expected to qualify more often than not.

I can't see Australia not being among the top four in the Asian World Cup qualifiers more often than not, though I warn we cannot and should not be complacent.

Make no mistake, Asia is still growing rapidly in terms of football. In particular China, who made the 2002 World Cup in Korea and Japan, is going to be a much greater force sooner rather than later. I visited China recently and was left stunned and speechless by what I saw. It is way ahead of Australia in terms of coaching (they have some of the best credentialed Yugoslav coaches), infrastructure, organization, facilities and passion.

That is why we have to be very careful that we don't rest on our laurels or make the same mistakes we did after the feats of the 1974 Socceroos. How many times were we told that the sleeping giant that was Australian soccer was now awake after what the '74 team achieved?

The sport was supposed to take off and challenge the other traditional football codes like AFL (then known as the VFL), rugby league and rugby union. History tells us it didn't happen for our game floundered for years on the ineptness of a long line of administrators who, while nearly all generally had good intentions in their hearts, were simply incapable of taking us to the next level.

What we needed was a bunch of fresh, young faces with fresh ideas and, most importantly, a plan and a vision. We didn't get it then and we didn't get it for some time after.

Maybe people think I am too tough on our administrators. Yes, they have a thankless task and have had to work under tough conditions, but no-one forced them to do it. They have a lot to answer for and I stand firm by my statements.

Until the Socceroos victory last year, I had been asked by thousands of people over the years why the game in this country had not gone ahead and why we hadn't qualified for the World Cup since 1974. Simple answer, really. Administration, or lack of it.

There were other factors as well. Certainly bad luck played some part, as did inept coaching while FIFA's kowtowing to the powerful football nations ensured the Socceroos were more often than not dealt unfair qualifying paths.

We should have capitalised on the 1974 Socceroos and set the game up for 100 years but Arthur George's mind had been poisoned. The English influence had reared its ugly head and he was now, in my opinion, a puppet for the likes of Englishman Eric Worthington.

Worthington's view of the football world was totally one-eyed. It was everything English and nothing else mattered. He had no vision in regards to what the rest of the football world was doing. He also had his boys and he did his best to look after them. But they were still babies in nappies in terms of coaching experience.

Even when Englishmen were not in the running for coaching positions, we had to endure the likes of German Rudi Gutendorf, who proved to be one of the great disasters when he was in charge of the Socceroos in the late 1970s, early 1980s. I lost count of the number of times I shook my head in shock and bewilderment at Gutendorf's methods.

He was at the helm when the Socceroos were beaten 2–0 by

New Zealand at the Sydney Cricket Ground in 1981 in one of the saddest moments I have had to endure. The Socceroos were diabolical as they were bundled out of contention for the 1982 World Cup finals.

They were booed off the ground and the media ripped in to them the next day. They lacked passion and leadership. You could tell they had had enough of Gutendorf. And so had Arthur as the German was sacked immediately and replaced by Les Scheinflug. Pity Arthur didn't sack himself for he was largely responsible for Gutendorf's appointment in the first place.

Look, we had the players to at least win the final stages of several World Cup qualifying campaigns, but they were let down by the men in charge.

Even though Worthington has long gone, we still seem to have a fascination and love affair with all things English when it comes to football. I believe it has held us back. Look at the various state academies. Englishmen are still heavily involved. You won't find that in Asia, Europe or South America. Look what has happened in England over the past eight to 10 years and at the men coaching in the premier league...Frenchmen, Spanish, Portuguese, Irish and Scottish. The big clubs are awake!

Another major problem for the game has been the soccer program at the Australian Institute of Sport. I know there are people who swear by it. They point to the players that have been produced like Frank Farina, Mark Viduka, Brett Emerton and Josip Skoko to name just a few.

However, I believe it has drifted away from what it was originally intended and that was as a means to help high performance national teams and coaches. Developing young athletes was not on the agenda. I should know because I was one of six people coopted to help form the AIS 25 years ago.

Early on it was good for the game because soccer had nothing else in terms of producing players, apart from various coaching clinics, many of which I was involved with!

Now, every state has a soccer academy and I don't believe the AIS is getting the best of talent. That's not to say the state academies are getting it right either because they are not. There does not seem to be a co-ordinated, simple plan to control the various programs. And some of those in charge are simply not the right people for the job. I was told a while ago that one coach was more interested in spending time on the golf course getting his handicap down than his job at a certain academy.

This is not the fault of the states that run the academies because there has to be direction from the top, the head body. But that could not happen because the ASF then Soccer Australia and now FFA have had the wrong people in charge as director of coaching.

We need someone like a Dr Josef Venglos, Gerard Houllier or Aime Jacquet. They are big names and coaches of substance and quality. They would provide wonderful guidance, knowledge and expertise to all coaches around the country.

A good case in point is Steve O'Connor, the head of the AIS soccer program. Steve has been in the job for some time and is a good, personable and educated man. He was a good player for the Socceroos and had a distinguished career in the NSL.

He hasn't done a bad job but imagine how much better he would be with someone like Venglos, Houllier or Jacquet to guide him.

That's why my eyes lit up when French World Cup winning coach Aime Jacquet visited Australia in February 2006 for a series of lectures involving coaches from all sports, not just soccer. Jacquet is one of the most celebrated coaches in the world, having guided France to their first World Cup finals victory in 1998 with one of the most talented sides I have seen.

Jacquet, who is exactly the type of person the FFA should be targeting as national director of coaching, made some very valid and pertinent points when he spoke to the media not long after his arrival in Australia, especially about developing our young players and coaches. Pivotal to all of that is a successful and strong national competition.

The A-League has, after just one season, been a wonderful success. It has drawn terrific crowds and the sort of media coverage that has been missing from the game for far too long.

Despite suggestions to the contrary, the standard of football is not better than the old National League and I would suggest that some of the great NSL sides of the 1970s and 1980s would beat most of the A-League clubs.

However, you cannot deny that the A-League is much better marketed and promoted and has far better media exposure on television and in radio and newspapers. A big plus is the fact that the Socceroos have qualified for the World Cup finals, sparking huge interest in the sport.

It will be interesting, however, to see how the League fares in its second season when the novelty has worn off and the harsh reality that running a football club in Australia, especially in soccer, is a costly, money-losing industry.

One of the major problems with the A-League is that it does not really cater to the development of young players. I know each club has to have a minimum of three players under the age of 20. However, that also hurts the clubs because they are limited by the size of their squads; they are allowed just 20 players, as it is. A few injuries and the coach might have to call on the youngster before he is really ready for the hurly burly of this standard of football.

The A-League needs a national under 20s youth league, just like it was in the now defunct National Soccer League. The youth league was a fantastic competition, a springboard not only to first team football but to the various age national teams, the Joeys (under 17s) and Young Socceroos (under 20s).

It is no coincidence that since the NSL was disbanded, thus leading to no more youth league, our performances at international youth level have been absolutely abysmal. It might also have something to do with the coaching. I'm sorry, but I can't see for the life of me how present youth coach, Ange Postecoglou, has held his job for more than six years.

My argument about a youth league was backed up in 2006 when the Australian under 17s failed to make it past the first stage of the Asian qualifiers for the World Youth under 17s championship. It was only the second time since 1985 that the under 17s have not competed at a World championship.

The Joeys were held to an 0–0 draw by Laos, then beat Indonesia 3–1 but were kicked out of the qualifiers because Laos, which beat Indonesia 5–0, had a better goal difference.

What a disaster. With all due respect, what has Laos done in world football at any level? How big is its population? How many registered players would it have? Do they even play with boots!

Compare Laos with the system and infrastructure in Australia, where we are swamped by academies all over the country. Obviously there is a huge problem somewhere. Certainly Postecoglou is not the man for the job and someone even higher than him must be held accountable.

I pose the question, 'Does anyone at the FFA have the knowledge and expertise to understand the requirements regarding the direction of football in this country'. It is not good enough to say that we have qualified for the World Cup finals so everything is fine.

Without good infrastructure, good coaching at junior level and the right people looking after our coaches, there is no future.

The youth teams have not reached anywhere near the level they attained under the guidance of one of the greatest youth coaches in the world, Les Scheinflug, whose record was phenomenal. Les took the under 19s twice to the World Youth cup semi-finals and took the under 17s to the final of the World Youth Championship in New Zealand in 1999, only to lose to Brazil in a penalty shoot-out after the scores were locked 0–0 after extra time.

At the time I described that achievement as one of the greatest in Australian soccer history and almost on the same par as the '74 Socceroos qualifying for the World Cup. Australia showed under Scheinflug that it can compete with the best junior sides in the world, but not lately.

Again, I get back to my argument about those in charge and having the right people—the Jacquets and Houlliers of this football world—guiding our coaches and players.

Thankfully, while we might have some issues regarding that area of the game, there is no such problem at the very top of the tree.

This is a new and exciting era for the game in Australia. The people at the helm, like Frank Lowy and John O'Neill, have done a wonderful job reinventing the game at administrative and football level. And it was there for all to see on Sunday, March 5, 2006, when almost 42,000 crammed into Aussie Stadium to watch Sydney FC beat the Central Coast Mariners 1–0 in the inaugural grand final of the national competition—the A-League.

What an occasion! I never thought I'd see such a reaction to a soccer club match in Australia. I was so proud to be there, to see the game so united, to see the fans, the families and the passion.

There is a new found respect and the media and general sporting public no longer looks on the sport with disdain. If there is one criticism I can make it is that maybe the FFA should involve some people with real football knowledge in administrative areas and some who have a good, working knowledge of our past.

But that is a small aside.

Australian soccer is going ahead and making a mark locally and internationally. I'd like to think I made a significant contribution, certainly more so than some of the administrators of the past.

Thanks From the Bottom of My Heart

Where do you begin to start to thank everyone who has played a special part in your life? The best place for me is my family. Being a parent is a difficult thing at the best of times, but when you are a sporting coach, particularly in football, it complicates matters even further. My life was consumed by football, both as a player and a coach, and, as a consequence, my family life suffered. It is something most professional coaches would understand.

I can only say to my son Simon and daughter Daniella, I love you so much and thank you for the sacrifices you had to put up with over the years. It saddens me that I wasn't at home enough to see you grow up during the most important times of your lives. But, despite that, you have turned in to wonderful people. I am so proud of you.

To the Australian Sporting Hall of Fame. What can I say? I am so privileged and honoured to be a part of your amazing family. You stand as a remarkable monument to the history and feats of so many Australian sportsmen and women. Is it any wonder tennis champion Roger Federer choked with emotion when he was presented to our sporting icon Rod Laver. Roger, now you know how I feel everytime I meet an Australian sporting great.

Coaching can be a very selfish and insular world, but I have been lucky to meet and work with some of the best all over the world—and not just in football. To those coaches who helped me and allowed me to learn from them and share ideas—I am indebted to you as I am to all the players I have been involved with at international and club level. One man I drew inspiration from was the legendary Rugby League coach Jack Gibson. What an incredible man and what an amazing character. As an Australian soccer administrator, John Barclay did so much for me. As a friend, he is forever in my heart. John was there when I arrived in Australia without a word of English. He was there when I got the job as state coach of Victoria, he was there when I became national coach and he was there when we went to the World Cup finals. Your loyalty over 40 years has been something very special to me.

The media has been an exceptional friend all over the world, but especially in Australia. Yes, there were some tough times and differences, but we always worked it out in the end. I still remain friends with many in the Australian media, especially the *Daily Telegraph's* John Taylor. We have not always seen eye to eye but I value John's opinion and his right to express them. It is a great sign of friendship when people can overcome differences and still be great mates.

Of course, where would I be without the Socceroos. We ARE a family. I would have achieved nothing without your help, support, encouragement and dedication. You have played such a big role in my life and I owe you everything. The years will take their-toll on us, but time will never diminish the love and respect I have for everyone of you. To the great Australian middle distance runner Ron Clarke and his wife Helen—your long time friendship (along with your late brother Jack Clarke) has been something I will always cherish. You are very special people to me as is Tony Rafty, the wonderful caricaturist, Edmund Parilo and the Scottish clan, who like to call me McRasic. Tony and Edmond's loyalty and vision have been simply wonderful.

The great Australian rules coach, Kevin Sheedy, is an extraordinary man who has survived in the cut-throat business of the AFL for so long and achieved so much success. He is a credit to coaching and a valued friend. To continually earn his praise over the years for my achievements is something that is truly special to me.

And what can I say about Ray Gatt, who helped me write this book? We have been mates for 20 years and you have helped me so much in terms of positive media. Thanks mate for putting up with my rantings and ravings, for your expertise, for the long hours you put into the book and, most of all, your frienship. Last and not least, to the kids of the world and the Australian sporting public...a huge thank you. The one million kids I have coached around the world in various clinics have helped me to feel eternally young. There have been fewer bigger thrills than seeing the smiles on the faces of the kids as they kicked the ball around without a worry in the world.

The sporting fans of Australia have been remarkable. Thank you for opening your hearts to me. Thank you for making me one of your own. Thank you for the thousands of cups of coffee I have shared with you all over the country in the name of Australia and football.

Rale Rasic

Index